WHAT IT MEANS
TO BE HUMAN

Other books in the Foundations of Christian Faith series

Christian Worship by Ronald P. Byars

The Trinity by Philip W. Butin

Searching for Truth by Thomas Currie

WHAT IT MEANS TO BE HUMAN

Living with Others before God

Michelle J. Bartel

Foundations of Christian Faith
Published by Geneva Press in Conjunction with
the Office of Theology and Worship, Presbyterian Church (U.S.A.)

Scripture quotations, unless otherwise indicated, are from the New Revised Standard Version of the Bible, copyright © 1989 by the Division of Christian Education of the National Council of the Churches of Christ in the U.S.A., and are used by permission.

Book design by Sharon Adams
Cover design by Night & Day Design

First edition
Published by Geneva Press
Louisville, Kentucky

This book is printed on acid-free paper that meets the American National Standards Institute Z39.48 standard. ∞

PRINTED IN THE UNITED STATES OF AMERICA

01 02 03 04 05 06 07 08 09 10—10 9 8 7 6 5 4 3 2 1

Library of Congress Cataloging-in-Publication Data

A catalog record for this book may be obtained from the Library of Congress.

ISBN 0-664-50164-8

Contents

Series Foreword

The books in the Foundations of Christian Faith series explore central elements of Christian belief. These books are intended for persons on the edge of faith as well as for those with strong Christian commitment. The writers are women and men of vital faith and keen intellect who know what it means to be an everyday Christian.

Each of the twelve books in the series focuses on a theme central to the Christian faith. The authors hope to encourage you as you grapple with the big, important issues that accompany our faith in God. Thus, Foundations of Christian Faith includes volumes on the Trinity, what it means to be human, worship and sacraments, Jesus Christ, the Bible, the Holy Spirit, the church, life as a Christian, political and social engagement, religious pluralism, creation and new creation, and dealing with suffering.

You may read one or two of the books that deal with issues you find particularly interesting, or you may wish to read them all in order to gain a deeper understanding of your faith. You may read the books by yourself or together with others. In any event, I trust that you will find a fuller awareness of the living God who is made known in Jesus Christ through the present power of the Holy Spirit. Christian faith is not about the mastery of ideas. It is about encountering the living God. It is my confident hope that this series of books will lead you more deeply into that encounter.

Charles Wiley
Office of Theology and Worship
Presbyterian Church (U.S.A.)

Acknowledgments

The privilege and pleasure of this writing project is that from start to finish it has been a community effort. First, thanks for the opportunity for the writing itself go to Charles Wiley, friend, colleague, and editor of the series who was gracious from beginning to end, bringing this vision for the church to fruition in careful editing and nurture. In addition I wish to thank the members of my writing group, Kathryn Cameron, Ron Byars, and Tom Currie, for their helpful feedback and insight. I am grateful to the other authors of the group who helped me think through these issues: it was a privilege to worship and work with them. Many thanks go to the Office of Theology and Worship of the Presbyterian Church (U.S.A.) for facilities, funding, and the call to the project itself. And I am grateful to those whose names I do not know who have contributed to the project.

Thanks for encouragement and patience go also to the Department of Religion and Philosophy at Augustana College, and to the congregation of Wild Flower Presbyterian Church, especially Suzy Smith and her family and the Buehlers, who all read the manuscript. Melissa Larsen and Andrew Johnson, research assistants at Augustana College, were also helpful conversation partners.

Most of all, I want to thank the members of my family, who have nurtured me into the image of God in and for which I was created. My parents and brothers and sister have been my loving friends and counsel for my whole life. My husband, Douglas Denné, has sustained me with gentleness, joy, and strength, making both the great and little details of this project possible.

Together Douglas and I offer this book as a gift in honor of the families to whom we are bound: the Crapuchetteses, Bartels, Dennés, Glunts, LaGrands, Carneys, Simses, Kearnses, Stories, and Justices; and together with love and prayer we dedicate this book to our nephews and nieces whom we celebrate as precious individuals in the image of God: Justin Storie, Devon Storie, Alexander Kearns, Shawn Denné, Donovan Kearns, John LaGrand, Jade Denné, Connor Kearns, Elizabeth Bartel, Isaac LaGrand, Alida Jane Bartel, Helen Joanne LaGrand, and all those whose names we do not yet know.

1

On Being Human

In the beginning . . . God created the heavens and the earth. . . . Then God said, "Let us make humankind in our image, according to our likeness."

*E*verything would be all right, said Dudley, "if only people could learn to behave like human beings." Wise words from an angel (Cary Grant in *The Bishop's Wife*—good casting to type, I say), truer to wisdom from our Christian tradition than the more common and more mistaken notion that problems exist because people, we say, "are only human."

Ah, the power of that "only"! What does it mean? It means that all we are is human, that we can't expect anything more, that human beings are creatures without inherent goodness or nobility, and that, when left to their human devices, people disappoint, frustrate, harm, and stray. It means that to be human is to be negligible. Invoking the "they're only human" clause when we sigh in resignation and shrug our shoulders at faulty behavior is to make two significant errors: To be human is defined by sin, and human sin is just the way things are.

Whenever Christians worship, however, they reject these errors. At the beginning of worship we gather around God because God has called us into the midst of the Divine. We are invited to gather with God in praise and adoration, and we are invited to be joined with the Holy Spirit in fellowship. This is an exercise in trust and confidence in the knowledge that this God is our God and can be trusted, because this God loves us with strong goodness. In our worship we also rely on the forgiveness of this God for our sins—sins that are so serious that they alienate us from ourselves, others, and the rest of creation, and sin so very present with us that we are utterly cut off from God. But in our worship services we hear the good news of the gospel that in Jesus Christ we are forgiven. The point of God's grace is precisely that sin does not define us. We are not defined by our actions, although these help us to become who we are. We are not defined by the world's definitions. We are not defined by the alienation we feel from God, nor by the anger we feel from or toward others. We're not defined by our romances, parenting, successes, trophies, or awards.

God Defines Us

So really, invoking the explanation that "they're only human" is only appropriate when a teacher sneaks a winter coat to that child in class with pale, bluish nails, or when the school janitor changes those nails to glowing pink when he gives up his gloves. Saying "they're only human" is appropriate when the shop owner laughs at the giggling child instead of reprimanding her, or when the librarian, instead of shushing the children, finds them more books to read to one another. This saying is appropriate when husbands and wives cook meals and do laundry for each other when the other is too weary. It is right and true to say "they're only human" when a youth group leaves on a trip to build a church for a group of people in need, or when the deacons visit anyone they can in a nursing home or hospital. "They're only human" when they run and play and think and cook and nurture and fix and teach and heal and solve simply because it is in them and they can. When humans are being their best then they are only, truly, magnificently human.

When humans give glory to God by excelling at who they have been created to be—by loving one another, by enjoying themselves and each other, by reaching out to one another in cooperation and service, by tending the earth, by participating in worship and fellowship, by embracing joy and forgiveness and generosity, by seeking the good of all in the good of each—then Dudley's words will find their prophetic fulfillment:

Everything would be all right if only people could learn to behave like human beings.

The Gift of the Garden

Of course, discovering the truth of what it means to be human and how to behave like a human being is a hard task. It's a mixed-up concept for us. Take sex, for instance. Our Christian tradition in so many ways denies sexuality as a basic ingredient of human life—something vulgar, at least, and evil, at worst. We don't teach sex (generally speaking) in a healthy way in our churches. But on the other hand, we'll write off affairs of unfaithful husbands by saying "boys will be boys," and we expect women to be sexy *and* chaste.

And sex is only one of the concepts we have that is so mixed up. Indeed, common confessions of sin in church services reflect our bewilderment about our own existence—we ask for forgiveness not only for what we have done, but also for what we have left undone. We hold up the sins we are aware of and the sins we commit without even being aware of them. We know we live in the midst of sin, that sins are not just particular acts. But we also know that Jesus Christ is with us, that God promises the Holy Spirit to be with us. In addition to knowing of our fallenness, we know also of our inherent goodness as creatures of God because God declared it to be so. We assert, we affirm, we believe that the truth of human existence is not in sin, but in its beginning in the garden. Our truth is with our Creator.

I must admit that when I was a child the Garden of Eden didn't interest me like it does now. This is because gardening, like hiking (more on that later), was one of those activities through which my parents tried to teach me life lessons (gardening didn't take, through no fault of their own). We had to weed the vegetable garden, which was a double downer for me since I enjoyed neither weeding in the dirt nor eating vegetables. I swore I would never have a garden (although swearing wasn't allowed either).

So when I heard about the Garden of Eden, I kept imagining a place that was no fun at all, hard work that would get in the way of lazing around and doing nothing, a place I had to be because my parents were trying to teach me something. I used to think of Eve as cranky because she had to weed.

Of course, I never would have said this out loud. I barely said it out loud to myself because surely, I thought, Eve wouldn't be cranky. This was, after all, before sin. So Eve would always have to be in a good mood. It wasn't until the first time I tried to teach the Garden of Eden story to college freshmen that the picture became clear to me.

So much had happened in the intervening years. I discovered I loved gardens. Not gardening, mind you, but gardens. I lived in England for a year and saw gardens beyond belief. With another friend from the states, I was wandering around Cambridge one day, and we walked by one of the college gardens. The gate posted a sign that said "Fellows Only. Closed to the public." We said "rats" and out of habit just tried the gate to make sure it was locked. It wasn't, and in we went, realizing, with a sneaky and sheepish giggle, that we Americans just don't have the same sense of propriety that our English friends at Cambridge possessed.

And it was beautiful. Gorgeous flowers of stunning color and shade. Bold, subtle, feathery, shouting, waving, scented, shy, the flowers and green leaves and grasses were like nothing I had ever seen. We had entered Narnia, and we both knew it, as the street sounds receded and we were left with the quiet rustling that cloaks a whole world. I have never looked at or listened to gardens the same way since.

Now I admire gardens, and what people do with them. I also admire gardeners. And although the extent of my gardening is a wildish herb garden, I have learned from my parents that nurturing beauty and truth and goodness, whether in a garden or in people, is very hard work, requiring effort from us when we do not want to give it, and persistence. And I have learned that the earth is a good thing and a delightful thing. Indeed, as much of a gardener as I am not, gardens and the Garden help me to understand the truth and beauty and goodness of my human life with God.

The story of Narnia, as C. S. Lewis records it in seven volumes, ends where it begins, only much, much better. Narnia is a place of such vivid fantasy it is real. It is full of truth, a kingdom full of the battle between good and evil, where earnest people strive toward peace and goodness. In Narnia, the new heaven and new earth are like the one we know, only good and true and beautiful. Narnia is where people exult and revel in peace and justice, not unlike the Peaceable Kingdom of so many artists' imaginations. The reconciling power of Aslan, the wild and good lion who represents Christ, is so strong and forgiving it welcomes the ones who are true followers even though their appearance is of the enemy. In the end, Narnia becomes as marvelous a place as it was in the beginning when evil was present, only better. Like Narnia, our Christian beliefs end where they begin, only much, much better, in a new heaven and a new earth where we see face to face, and not through a glass darkly. Our hope is not in an eradication of this world, but in the saving and restoring of it.

So one of my goals is to convince freshmen of this notion of the Garden of Eden as an indication of the truth of the goodness of God. Every semester they want to tell me that we need to have sin so life is interesting and not boring as with Adam and Eve. "Boring?" I say. "You call it boring walking around buck naked in a garden full of fruit and flowers and pure water and having sex with that other person there with you and Labrador retrievers wherever you look, frolicking around?" (I teach in South Dakota, and my students skip class to hunt.)

How bewildered and misguided have we become if we think goodness and fun are mutually exclusive? That delight and interest and revelry are not a good part of what it means to be human? That earthiness is not part of our true human nature?

Gardens bring humans and the earth together in an effort for food and feasting and beauty. When we commune with nature—in whatever way we do—we join in the community of Adam and Eve with each other and the garden and God. God placed them together, in the garden, where the Creator was divinely present in the very center. That Adam and Eve were created by God and placed in the garden, which was God's gift to them for their enjoyment, is not just a pretty fairy tale. It is fundamental to our Christian understanding of being human. But before we dig into this more, we need to see where the rubber hits the road. Because a human isn't an idea. A human is a real person.

A Person

One of the most astounding events I ever witnessed was the birth of my first nephew. I didn't actually witness the birth—thank goodness, because it was a Cesarean section, and I'm not known for my ability to stomach such things—but what I did witness was an amazing transformation. What had been my sister with a huge stomach became my sister and another person. What had been a lump was now a person. The doctors reached in and pulled out . . . a person. This person—that newborn baby—has grown into a lovely, fun, beautiful, intelligent, and sensitive boy who loves all things pirate and hates it when squirrels get hurt, and who has his very own place in my heart.

It was as though this person came from nowhere. Of course, you ask my sister and she'll tell you that he very definitely came from her, that he was very definitely present, for nine very long months. But how is it possible that the basic biological process of procreation can produce a person? Not just a mechanical replication, but a being with independence, with thoughts, feelings, characteristics, faults, struggles, creativity, humor, delight? A person, we realize when we think about it, can never come from us alone, even if we fertilize the egg in a test tube, even if we clone. All we do is assemble the parts, even if we do it the old-fashioned way. We can't make a *person* on our own, because if we could, that person would be no different from a bench or a cake or a vase: a thing, an object, an article, that has no life of its own. All we do is start the process. The person, the existence of that being that finally remains apart from us, his or her very own being, comes from somewhere else that we can't control.

That is why, I imagine, the psalmist writes "before I was born you knew me," and "I have been wonderfully and fearfully made." And that is why the psalmist asks with great earnestness, "What are human beings that you are mindful of them?" For how can God, the Creator of persons, beyond us, more than us, be mindful of these earthly creatures? But this is exactly what we believe; in fact, it is the good news of the gospel. As Christians we affirm that God is mindful of us, loves us, created us, redeemed us, sustains us.

Some of us feel it, and believe it deeply, deep in our bones, and in our souls. Some of us doubt constantly that we are worthy of God. We doubt God's use for us. We feel and think that we have sinned so despicably as to remove ourselves from God's good graces, from God's safe presence, from God's own work. We have disappointed and been disappointed. Our work feels meaningless. Our lives are stressful. We can't make ends meet. We own so many things we are obsessed with acquiring more and protecting what we've got. We don't understand our children.

But friends, this is the good news of the gospel. In Jesus Christ we are forgiven. And what we as Christians affirm is that this forgiveness—the work of grace—is free and clear and that we are restored as God's created and called people to God's presence. We have always been God's beloved children—this has never changed. There is nothing we can do to make God love us more, and there is nothing we can do to make God love us less.

We believe that we were, and are, created in the image of God. And what we will discover, as we study biblical passages and engage in conversation with Christian theology throughout this book, is that being created in the image of God *is not something we can change*. We cannot sin it away. What good news! No matter how we live, no matter what we do, no matter our heartbreaks and triumphs and joys and loves, we will always be people created in the image of God. That transformation from lump to person that I witnessed in the birth of John was only a transformation in *my* eyes: In God's eyes, John always was and always will be God's child, created in God's image, for God's good purpose and pure joy.

Being Human, Being Created
in the Image of God

What does it mean to be human? In this volume we will take this question to heart. As we explore this question, we need to think about why we are asking it and what we hope to get out of asking such a question. As Christians we believe that people are created by God. But what does it mean to be created *by God?* What is it that God has created? Even if we fully understand what it means to be created by God, does this affect our day-to-day life as Christians?

People ask questions about being human for many reasons. Sometimes our questions are prompted by growing up. When a fourteen-year-old asks, "Why did God put me on this earth anyway?" she poses the question with clarity and urgency. And this questioning about the meaning of our lives doesn't stop with adolescence. The midlife crisis often results when a forty-year-old man finds himself looking back at his life and wondering, "What has it all been for?" As we grow we ask questions about what our life means, and what our purpose is.

Others ask the question because of heartbreak, depression, and struggle. Still others ask these questions, not for themselves, but for others: "Surely a child molester is not human." Or Christians may assume that being created in the image of God is true only for confessing Christians and not for others.

And as people struggle through various crises in their lives, they ask the question of what God wants for them. "Am I special?" "Do I have anything worthwhile to offer?" "I'm only sixteen. I can't get a good job. What good am I?" "I'm gray and not as spry as I used to be. My memory is fading. Is my vocation over and done with? Am I past my use?" "Am I more than a collection of genes?"

As important as these questions are, they cannot be answered by isolated individuals on solo quests to find themselves. When the Bible speaks of what it means to be human, it does so within the context of community. In the New Testament the word commonly used for community is *koinonia*. What makes us human in koinonia is that we fulfill ourselves through giving ourselves to God and others, a love of neighbor and self rooted in the love of the self-giving triune God who is love itself. We grow up as we learn to build each other up through giving of ourselves. In such an environment, we do not lose our individuality; rather, our individuality is achieved and expressed through relating to others. We give of ourselves to one another for the sake of one another, as a mother nurses her child and a daughter cares for her aging mother.

Our generosity and self-giving to one another is fundamentally a response to God's own generosity to us. Christ's generous gift to us was the gift of service:

> ... who, though he was in the form of God, did not regard equality with God as something to be exploited, but emptied himself, taking the form of a slave, being born in human likeness. (Phil. 2:6–8)

Jesus modeled equality to God, we read in Philippians 2, not by lording it over others or dominating others, but by taking on the form of a servant, and pouring himself forth for the sake of others. In our response to that gift, we do not just consider ourselves "changed" or "saved" on our own, but, following Christ's example, we pour out ourselves for one another. Christ, in this pouring out for others, actually creates a new community, a new society of individuals together for one another, a church where we learn to live in community.

Human beings are fundamentally connected, to God and to one another. We learn to be human along with other folks who are learning to be human. Being human means day-to-day life where we learn to make decisions and live out attitudes and beliefs. Being human means being anchored and guided by God. Being human means worship, learning to live out our baptism, and sharing the bread and cup.

Being human means being created in the image of God, by God, out of God's desire and decision to do so. The story of creation begins the telling of our Christian faith, and includes an understanding of our human existence in the midst of this world.

How did this one phrase from Genesis—"Let us make humankind in our image, according to our likeness"—become so important to the Christian tradition? The concept of the *imago Dei* (Latin for "the image of God") was a concept used by the early church to help them understand their relationship with Christ. Christ is the very image of God and truly human, the New Testament tells us. This ancient phrase—*imago Dei*—used throughout the life of the Christian church helps us to plumb the depths of what it means to be human in relationship to God through Christ.

Christians' understanding about being human comes from what

we learn about Jesus Christ, who we affirm is fully God and fully human. Believers in the early church spoke about being created in the image of God because of their connection to Christ. Studying the belief that we are created in the image of God will help us to articulate what our call is as human beings. Examining what it means to be human will help us to understand the nature of the human vocation in the midst of the world in which God has placed us. And we will see that we need to be more humble than we tend to think.

In addition, studying this concept will help us to understand what our everyday lives can be like, since being created in the image of God is directly related to what God wills for human life. Without exploring this, we will not be able to grasp what it means to be and live in relationship with God.

What Is an Image?

Is an image a reflection, like a mirror? Is it a representation, as in art or music? Is it a description, as in philosophy, theology, or literature? When we use the term "image," many meanings come to mind. In our culture, we constantly discuss self-image. As a society, we think that how we feel about ourselves is vital to our well-being. Magazines, commercials, television, and cinema all encourage us to have a good self-image. And our culture constantly provides ways for us to have a good self-image. People want us to buy exercise equipment, use makeup, wear the right clothes, live in the right houses, promising that we will then feel good about ourselves. Dave Barry writes that when we listen to these people we're trying to look like people who don't look like people. Interesting, isn't it, that not only do various organizations and corporations want us to have a good self-image, but they can tell us what that self-image should be. So is it really a *self*-image?

"Image" also refers to the way we communicate. To say that someone isn't very graceful, that they are "like a bull in a china shop," is to say that they are a klutz. That image works. Or to say that someone took good care of me, that he's "a regular Florence Nightingale," is to describe someone's strength and compassion in caring. Muhammad Ali said he "danced like a butterfly, and stung like a bee."

So images communicate ideas, meaning, and depth. Images convey something to us that we would not understand otherwise, by clarifying or deepening our understanding. To use an image is to make something our own, to make it part of our understanding. That is why pictures of loved ones are so valuable to us: they bring us just a little bit of that person that we can hold on to. I never figured that I would be the kind of person to go nuts about our puppy. But I have—and I take four little photo albums with me when I travel so my friends can see her. What's more amazing is that my friends ask to see the pictures and seem to enjoy them. The reason they do is because they understand how much I enjoy my puppy, and that she is an important part of my life. (And how's this for an image, an image of contentment and companionship? My seven-pound, four-month-old puppy is curled up in a little white furball under my chair, sleeping, as I write at my computer.) Pictures, paintings, drawings, sculptures all bring something real to our imaginations, minds, and hearts. They are not the thing itself, but they evoke from us experience of something, they make real an understanding or impression. When we listen to music, it brings us images of dances, waltzes, planets exploding into existence, a sweet woman, a floating cloud, a battle, a choir of heavenly angels. Music moves us because it expresses the emotions we feel, and when the intensity of our life is unspeakable, music articulates the core of our being.

Television and movies are full of images. There is even a Museum of the Moving Image. These images show us families, lifestyles, experiences, morality, love, work, competition, and a host of other experiences and "realities." This is perhaps the greatest challenge for Christians in thinking about being created in the "image of God." For the images that we know on a day-to-day basis are flat, unreal, fictional, unreachable, distant, but ever-present, forceful, and dominant. Many people think that *The Simpsons* is one of the funniest shows ever. But do we see ourselves in the images of Homer, Marge, Lisa, or Bart? Is Frazier the kind of person I want to be? Is his apartment the kind I need to have in order to be socially acceptable (personally, I hope it's Niles's apartment!)? Is the proper role of men that of defensive linemen and the proper role of women cheerleaders? Or is the proper role of women that of soccer world champions and the proper role of men that of loving family men?

Television and movies not only bind, they can help us to explore new ideas, new images, new ways of humor, love, work, and family. When we think about them while we enjoy them, these and other art forms can be seen as expressions of human struggle with and delight in human existence. To see a husband and wife on a sitcom actually working through a problem builds up possibilities for the strengthening of love. And we learn how to make jokes along the way. A movie can convey to us the struggle of good against evil and give us an example of how one person battles mightily through an alcohol addiction for a good that prospers human life. Aristotle, long ago, observed that we learn virtues through habits, through learning how to do things in the right way at the right time. The important thing is not just having habits, or customs. It makes all the difference which ones you have.

What this vast array of images forces us to consider is the necessity, not of banning some images and exalting others, but of learning how to perceive and ponder images. We must learn how to question the images set before us. The early reformers banished absolutely all images from churches, not because images in and of themselves were bad, but because these reformers found that the images themselves were being worshiped as gods. Instead of helping people to worship the one true living God, pictures took the gaze of the people away from God. This didn't begin with the Reformation. We read in the Old Testament of Moses' dismay when he came down from Mount Sinai with the Ten Commandments, only to find the people (God's chosen people) making idols, making gold images, to substitute for the awesome, powerful, mighty God who created them. They tried to make God something tangible, something less than what God was, something they could control.

Problems We Face

One of the themes played out in our culture on a daily basis is "self-construction": the idea is that we can create ourselves into the particular selves we want to be. In everything from ads for fitness machines, clothing, makeup, and cars, to the schemes of pop psychology and talk-show hosts to make us rich and happy and "spiritual," we are told that we can create ourselves and make ourselves who we want to be. Usually, we are told that who we want to be is thin and fit (like the people in TV who look exactly like each other) and rich, with perfect families of four or five with a dog (usually a golden retriever or a setter) leaping into the boat with us, a boat docked at the edge of a small, pristine lake at the edge of which is a very large, warmly lit, beautifully landscaped home, with a grandparent walking down from the huge, well-furnished (with wicker and teak) wraparound porch, holding a mug of coffee, past the factory-perfect SUV to send the family fishing expedition off on a gentle glide across the still, serene lake.

Not that there's anything wrong with that picture! The problem is when one standard becomes a standard that society expects all its members to achieve. For decades we have become aware of the close connection in our society between being consumers and being Christians. We have so closely identified being good and pure with being rewarded in material and financial ways that we place a huge and ultimately greedy burden on ourselves to make ourselves into what we are told we should be. Freedom, in our modern mind-set, is linked directly and definitively to economics, whether we realize it or not. We Christians shrug our shoulders at those who get what they want, even if it hurts people economically or otherwise, because they did everything within the system. "They worked the system to their advantage," we say, and applaud them for their ingenuity and guts. That's what it means to be an American.

But we have arrived at a point where many people feel vaguely uneasy about something in our capitalist culture. We've been told we're products, not persons. Some people find themselves uncomfortable with waste, and so they recycle. Some people find themselves uncomfortable with greed, and so they slow down. We have a vague uneasiness about the existence of vehicles that are dangerous to small cars, horrendous wasters of natural resources, and terribly expensive, but are a status symbol anyway. In the midst of this, we, as Christians, have to face the fact that the image in which we are created is the image of God. And God is not the same as America. God is not the same as capitalism. God is not the same as things. God is not the same as us.

Our source of life is not capitalist success; it is not the American dream. What makes our human life good is not these things, but the God of our life. What we Christians must remember is that we are *created*. We do not create ourselves. We do not bring ourselves into existence. The power of life may be one we can manipulate to a degree (although we have limited understanding of the implications of processes like cloning or the limits of gene therapy), but the power of life is not one we own or control. We only participate in this preexistent power. So of what use for us are the exercises of self-construction? What do we gain if we purchase the right things and display the correct lifestyle and image? Of what good is it that we are associated with the right class, the right kind of people? "For what will it profit them to gain the whole world and forfeit their life?" (Mark 8:36.) If we are created, what do we do to ourselves and to each other if we usurp the role of Creator? Why do we want to be God?

Much has been written about the malaise of our consumerist culture. Perhaps the most prominent studies focus on the effect on women. A few years ago studies observed that the only ten-year-old girls that did not diet and didn't think of themselves as fat were athletes. Anorexia and bulimia are still quite common. Stories still abound on news programs helping women to balance their lives of being full-time mothers and full-time workers: Usually they are told they can find sanity by buying exercise equipment so that their self-image doesn't suffer from the effects of age (oh, the horror!), a tragedy that can also be stopped with creams. Stories about neglect of children focus almost entirely on the mothers of these children, with no mention at all of the absent fathers.

But men are burdened as well. In sitcoms and commercials shown during "women's shows" and sporting events, men are sometimes portrayed as kind and good, but almost always as stupid and boorish and clueless. Men, we are told, have no innate instincts for love, maturity, conversation, growth, or wisdom about being human. Women are never in the wrong, according to television, when it comes to issues of the family. Men need them as teachers. Men are the rough—very rough—*semi*-precious gems that are patiently (and manipulatively) polished by their women. Men are to know everything about cars, machines, sports, romance; men are to be strong and fit and funny.

So many people suffer that all sorts of entrepreneurs have begun to use this malaise with which they have infected our society as a new consumer base. New products and programs are popping up all the time to help people feel better about themselves and to find ways to create the image of themselves that they want to create. Even the seemingly benign movement toward creating the kind of spirituality that's best for you is a consumer endeavor as you pick and choose from the vast array of spiritual options available. Our economic and social lives become focused inward, and isolated individualism has become encouraged. Of course, with so many people suffering on so many levels, it is difficult to see whether the problems with image begin with society, media, or ourselves.

The resolution, of course, is of the chicken-and-egg variety: we could begin anywhere. But we cannot resolve the dilemma of the heartache, abysmal self-esteem, neglect of others, and narcissism of our culture by finding the problem and fixing it. We end up in one of those scenes in movies in which someone is having a fit, and they are slapped into sense. But the good news of the gospel for all whom God has created is that we are not merely having a fit, and God does not slap us into sense. God is just and generous, merciful and fierce, loving and a teacher, challenging and a friend. The responsibility for resolving this dilemma is not to control how it works out, but to open ourselves to God's presence as provident and saving Creator, here and now, in our society, in our lives. This is the presence of a living God, we believe, who showed in the incarnate life, death, and resurrection of Jesus Christ that God does not come to the world to condemn it, to merely slap it into sense, but to save it.

The real trick is to discern how to open ourselves up to God. It sounds very nice to say "Let go and let God," but that is vague and unhelpful when your teenage daughter screams at you because you eat steak. It is unhelpful when your coworkers encourage you to take steps that are legal but unethical. It is discouraging when you try to teach your son that his age and the color of his skin are going to shout to the white world that he is a drug dealer and rapist when he is really decent and blossoming as a future musician and father. It is unhelpful when your aging parent cannot function on her own but cannot give up her independence. How do we go about recognizing the living and present God as *our* Creator, and how do we go about actual everyday life making this manifest? In other words, how do we go about our lives in gratitude for being created by the God who loves us, and how do we live in openness to God's continuing creative work?

As Christians we know we are to be in the world but not of it. This is the world, society, and culture we are in. How do we live *in* it and *for* it while being *of* God? In the end we can only be for the world and for one another if we are of God. We can rest assured that God knows our struggle, and God calls believers to follow in this time and place, for "indeed, God did not send the Son into the world to condemn the world, but in order that the world might be saved through him" (John 3:17). While our current society presents problems for being human, there do exist unique opportunities for insight as we think through these problems. Ultimately, this is due to the fact that, for Christians, to be human is *good*. To be human is to be loved, and called, and created, not by humans, but by God who is present with us in this society and who is beyond this society.

We experience pain and suffering when we try to create ourselves and others, and the Christian's response to this goes to the depth of what it means to be human. The Christian response to the heartache, suffering, and oppression is a response that doesn't stop pain, but does stop disintegration. The good news of the gospel is not that heartache will cease, but that futility will. God promises us that God's words will not return empty. Our actions and deeds and loves are good and fruitful not because of how well we do them, but because they are done in the midst of God's work in the world. Indeed, they *are* God's work in the world. God is the one who, according to one translation of Romans 8:28, "makes everything work together for good." We are promised in the good news that we are precious, because God has said so, not because others have. We are promised that we are held in God's hands, not because we bargained for it, but because God has already placed us there, picked us up, and cradled us. The goodness of being human has already been established. And we are promised that it is God's passionate and loving desire that is waiting for our embrace. To be whole does not mean to find the right program, possession, stock portfolio, spouse, or house. To be whole does not mean to be a thing, but to be created by God. To be human, to be whole, means to live with God and with others, to live as a created being with the Creator and the rest of creation.

And the blessed, joyous surprise of the gospel is that this is *real* life. This is not getting our theological ducks in a row, although that is important. It is not making the exact right decisions at every turn, although that is important. It is not the profound insight or earth-shattering experience, although these are certainly part of being human. But Christians need to remember that being human is both an everyday and an extraordinary good, because God said it is, and lived this declaration in the incarnation of Jesus Christ; and it is everyday life, tilling the garden, walking in the garden, eating and talking in the garden. Being human is small things and big things. It is ripe fruit and broken romances, it is a loved baby with genetic defects and a lost job. It is huge mistakes and jokes that bind friends. Living as a created being with the Creator and the rest of creation is mundane diaper-changing and a job as a janitor. It is shared fun at a football game and shared sublimity at a musical performance. It is hurting someone's feelings and reconciling. It is quiet observation of your child embracing a flower and loud observation of your spouse getting an award. It is conversation during meal preparation and it is receiving a diagnosis of cancer. It is searching for purpose and finding one's call as a nurse's assistant.

Our search is not futile, either. Like every other generation we are receivers of the promise of God found in Jeremiah: "When you search for me," says our God, "you will find me" (Jer. 29:13). We must listen to the call of God to come back from going astray, as each generation must. Like our spiritual forbears, we are in an exile of a sort, like Jeremiah in Babylon. The word of God through Jeremiah was a word of the richness and abundance of life, a call that even though they were exiled in Babylon, still they should marry and have children, build houses and plant gardens. This life is not a punishment, but a gift. God calls us to a life of joy and generosity, not selfishness and stinginess. Our life is a life for God, for ourselves, and for others.

2

Human Being in the Image of God

So, does the angel Dudley in *The Bishop's Wife* have any biblical basis for saying that the world would be all right if only
everyone behaved like human beings? Yes, he does. (He's an
angel, after all.) So many of the struggles between God and
human beings arise when human beings go their own way, in
a direction away from God. Even though they belong to the
Divine, the people of God assert their ability to live as though
they didn't need the Creator, the one to whom they are bound
in their very being. If being human is to be bound to, with,
and for others and God, then the exhortations of the prophets
and others in the Bible make all the sense in the world. The
rejection of the poor, the desire for personal gain, undertaking the rituals of worship simply for the sake of getting the
task done, all mean that people have rejected God as an intimate part of their lives.

What does it mean to be human? Who are the creatures
that God created human beings to be? What is human life all
about? Adam and Eve in the Garden of Eden had all sorts of
gifts to be human, right there in the garden. They had the
earth and all creation that was theirs to play freely in, in
which to have dominion and subdue the earth. They had each
other. And in the garden they had two trees that helped them
to know the lay of the land; the tree of life, and the tree of the
knowledge of good and evil. The garden was the place they
communed with God, each other, and nature itself.

During our recent spring break my husband and I took our
little dog Tuck over to the campus, since we knew few students

would be around and she could run freely—because Tuck simply cannot restrain herself from trying to jump into anyone's arms and lick them until they know they're loved (she's terribly, wonderfully, indiscriminate). What a marvelous time! The air was warm and soft, and the few students out there were playing a round of Frisbee golf, enjoying the weather, each other, and the manic white fluff ball running toward them. They made her day and she made them smile— she licked them until they knew they had a friend for life.

Moments like these are wonderful gifts to college professors, because they put the times of struggles between teachers, students, and institution into proper perspective. I am the last person to tell my students that unless they get A's, they will have no chance for success. (I still can't believe how patient my parents were with my semester of 1.07 during my college years.) I even managed to muff up seminary courses to the tune of a couple of D's. Yet, here I am, in work I enjoy. But no matter how much I assure my students that their success and happiness in life do not depend on one grade, the tension still exists, because we feel like we are at odds. Now don't get me wrong: classrooms are not battlegrounds. But there is still a way in which professors have power that students don't have.

So when we strolled across the green and everything and everyone touched by the soft, warm sun was exuding peace and delight, the professor and the student and the spouse and the dog could all just be, in peace and delight with one another.

It was the Peaceable Kingdom. It was human life at its best and we were *blessed*. Someday, I know, the power of professors and students will only and always be for the other, for their sake, and for the sake of their common pursuit of truth. For now, we college folks see through a glass darkly and only in part. But when we have a glimpse of that deep sense that our life is a life for God, for ourselves, and for others, then we can see that the "Peaceable Kingdom" is nearly a perfect summary of the Christian idea that human beings are created in the image of God.

But our thinking on these ideas often starts moving away from blessing and toward curse, at least toward life under curse, life outside the garden, life lived in fear and shame and guilt before our God. One of the frustrations in talking about this doctrine (or "teaching") of the church is that we get in our minds an image of what it must mean to be a "perfect" person. "If I am created in the image of God," we think, "then I am falling way, way short." Because to our minds, to be in the image of God means that we must be perfect.

But yet another news item in the proclamation of the good news of the gospel is that being fully human is *not* being God. We are creatures, not Creator, so being created in the image of God does not mean we have to be just like God. We are human, earthly and earthy beings, walking the ground underneath our feet, picking flowers, eating fruit, throwing baseballs, digging garden plots. To be fully human is not to be just like God, but to be human. And our true nature is seen not in our sinfulness, but in the fact that God called us into existence and created us in the blessedness of true relationship with God and others. Sin, as the sixteenth-century theologian John Calvin puts it, *deranges* our nature. It takes the God-given arrangement and messes it up.

It's almost easier to get a sense of being created to be human by starting from the end of the Christian Bible and looking backward. The apostle Paul spoke often and eloquently about Christian maturity, about how life should be lived and why it should be lived that way. In Ephesians and in other letters Paul writes of what it means to be the body of Christ, and he notes one thing in particular that we should not miss.

> But speaking the truth in love, we must grow up in every way into him who is the head, into Christ, from whom the whole body, joined and knit together by every ligament with which it is equipped, as each part is working properly, promotes the body's growth in building itself up in love. (Eph. 4:15–16)

Paul takes great pains to point out that to be a human being in a Christian understanding means to be part of a community. The nature of this community is like a human body: Every individual element, or member, of the body is crucial for the body to be whole, and it is also crucial for each and every member of the body to be functioning well for the body, as a whole, to be healthy. This is what Paul Lehmann, a theological ethicist of recent years, called "the good of all in the good of each." In other words, to be fully human means to be a unique, healthy, functioning individual in the body of Christ, which means that we cannot be unique, healthy, and functioning unless we are members of the community.

Christian maturity, in other words, is not seen in individuals standing alone, but in the togetherness of individuals. We grow and mature together—we cannot, in Christian terms, mature on our own. Christian maturity—or full humanity—is marked not by being perfect but by being a part of the community. Lehmann has another wonderful phrase that expresses our relationships to one another as individuals who are all part of the same body: "self-acceptance through self-giving." We make each other unique, healthy, and functioning through giving of ourselves to the other person and receiving the gifts of others. It is impossible, as a solitary, isolated human being, to reflect the image of God. We do this only in community.

Community in the Garden

It is in the book of Genesis that we find the first indication of what the apostle Paul is talking about. In Genesis (which means "beginning" or "origin") we read of the creation of human beings after the creation of everything else. Light and dark, sky and sea, earth and water, animals and plants have all been created, and into this world God calls a new creature, human being.

> Then God said, "Let us make humankind in our image, according to our likeness; and let them have dominion over the fish of the sea, and over the birds of the air, and over the cattle, and over all the wild animals of the earth, and over every creeping thing that creeps upon the earth." So God created humankind in his image, in the image of God he created them; male and female he created them. (Gen. 1:26–27)

The creation of humankind is the creation of two people, together, and two different people at that. To be human means to be more than one, and these humans are created for dominion over God's earth. Two people who are different from one another, male and female. Adam and Eve, man and woman, together, are the image of God. These human beings are created, and blessed, and placed very firmly in the rest of creation, in a fruitful garden given to them for their prosperity.

This passage can help us to understand some of the questions we have. Why did God create human beings? Why does God care about me and love me? Am I worthwhile? Is my relationship to God conditional? How do I know I belong to God? What is my relationship to other human beings? Is reflecting the image of God something I am commanded to do? What does being created as human mean about my relationship to the rest of creation, like the earth, and plants and animals?

And these are just a few of the questions that we ask!

Humans, Beings Created by God

Oftentimes people who are not Christians and who affirm no particular religious commitment still use the word "creation" to refer to the earth and nature. But for Christians, using the words "Creator," "create," "creature," and "creation" means something very particular. It means that to be human, to be made of stuff, to be made at all, means that we believe *something or someone made us*. This means that our existence depends on something or someone beyond ourselves.

As Christians we believe that this is God, the Creator of all that is. All that is, including us, and including the rest of nature, is dependent on God for its existence. God is the one who chooses us because God is the one who creates us, on whom we depend for our very existence. In fact, it's part of being human to be connected to the Divine by this Creator-creature relationship. And this means that God is the One we depend on, the ground of all our life.

We also see from the first three chapters in Genesis that God *chose* to create human beings in God's image. So the God *in whose image* we are created is a God of freedom, choice, and relationship. Somehow we are like this God: we mirror this God in some way; in some way we represent this God on earth.

The thing is, this representation is not a static one, or a passive one. To be an "image" is so often thought to be a picture, like on a wall. But you'll remember in the first chapter that I discussed the *creating* of images, that we strive to become something. This, of course, I pointed out as a negative. The opposite of the futility of our self-creation without God, however, is the fruitfulness of God continuing to create us. My Jewish colleague puts it this way: we are in the imagining of God. If the meaning of the Hebrew language of Genesis is taken seriously, then human beings, alone of all God's creatures, are created out of the very imagination of the Divine, from deep inside God's heart and mind and soul. Human beings, then, are part of God, yet distinct from God. They are connected to the life of the Divine, yet distinct from it.

Not unlike parents and children, my colleague pointed out, for when you parent children, whether they became your children through birth or adoption, they bear your image. They carry your mannerisms, maybe they look like you. But most important, he pointed out, is that your life has been caught up irrevocably in theirs. When they hurt, you yourself hurt. They are yours, your beloved children whom you have named and called your own, but they have become engrafted into your very being. They are an extension of you, but not you.

When I was a baby, I had a fairly serious ear infection, having woken up one morning with my ear sticking out from my head at a funny angle. So my parents took me to a doctor, found out I had a mastoid infection, and quickly administered antibiotics. Mom and Dad were told that if something didn't change that day, I would have to be admitted to the hospital that evening. Kind of scary for a parent, especially when you know that sort of infection had killed children just a decade or two earlier. Mom and Dad have never really talked about it, though, because everything turned out OK (although they bring up the joke my grandfather cracked, pointing out that they would always be wondering if I was really listening. Ha-ha). Then, about ten years ago, we woke up to our cat screaming in the basement, otherworldly scream-howls that were terrifying. Dad tried to see if he could help her, but she was clearly over the edge of cat sanity and was attacking things that weren't there. As we waited helplessly upstairs, I said to Dad how horrible it was to know she was in such devastating pain, and we could do nothing for her. "Not as bad as when it's your one-year-old child," he said. I got a glimpse then of what it is like to have a child. When they suffer, you suffer, and it's made so much worse when you can't communicate, because this person whom you love and cherish needs you and depends on you.

We are completely dependent upon God for our existence, which is the same thing as saying that being human is a state completely dependent upon God. We cannot be human without being connected to God, and being upheld by God's imagination. These two thoughts go hand in hand, and we see them very clearly in the creation story. How does God create human beings in Genesis 1? By God's word. When God says, something is.

This is different from the way our human words work. When a mom tells her child, "Clean up your room," that room does not automatically get cleaned up. A long process is involved. The child points out that "it will just get messy again anyway." Besides, the child adds, "It's too hard to get my room really clean." Then that long-suffering mother has to convince her child that "clean" means that clothes are actually put away, and not just piled in the hallway.

However, when God says . . . it is! God calls all sorts of things into existence by God's word: light and dark, earth, sea, and sky, day and night, fish, birds, flowers, animals, and human beings. God says, "Let us make human beings in our image." And there they are. As Christians we believe that what connects us to God is the word of God. "Word" here does not mean simply an idea or a proposition. When we read in the Bible that God speaks, we understand that God brings people together with God and with each other. In this way, God's word is much more like a conversation which creates relationships and community, because God speaks to us.

This is not unlike the way people nurture love between themselves. When we love someone else, we do all sorts of things for them and with them. But we also tell them we love them, and this helps strengthen what exists. Or think about those times when you first start falling for someone. We get all coy, pass notes if we're in school, talk to our friends, wonder, "Does he really like me? Is she really interested in me?" And then one day it becomes clear when that person says "I love you" or "I really want to spend some time with you." These words create a new reality by changing our understanding of what's going on.

God's power of speech is infinitely more powerful than ours—and infinitely more loving. God creates community because God is love (1 John). So when God calls human beings into existence—as two people together—God also creates connection, community, and relationship. God gives life.

None of these other things that God had created represented God on earth—not fish, flowers, rocks, or even little white puppies. All of these things, fulfilling their existence in their individual beauty and purpose, glorify God simply by being. But God wants love and glory and fulfillment to be freely returned. So when God creates human beings, God creates beings that are free in relationship to the Divine. The rest of nature does not have that freedom. Humanity brings with it the Creator's own freedom—freedom to be for God like God is for us. This is the image of God in which we are created. We reflect this divine image by being for God and for others, just as God chooses to be for us in creating us. All creation is good, not because it is inherently worthy, or is the best possible world, but because God chooses to be in relationship with it. It is the one which God chooses to bring into existence.

There's even another, more vivid, image from Genesis, in another section that tells about the creation of human beings. In Genesis 2, we read of God digging in the dirt and forming a human being, Adam, and breathing life into him. Think of yourself—or a child you know—who digs in dirt for whatever reason. Are you a gardener? A potter? Think of what you create. Think of planting seeds—taking something from a dead-looking seed and watering it and weeding it until it grows big and strong and fruitful and produces those lovely flowers or sun-ripened tomatoes that are so sweet they taste almost like candy. Or think of a potter who takes clay and turns it into something beautiful and useful. This is the image the writer of Genesis gives us, dirt and clay and muddy hands.

God breathed life into it. We humans can only rearrange elements. We can't take something dead and bring life back into it.

God breathes life into dirt. And then God—because it is not good that Adam is alone—puts Adam to sleep, and takes some flesh and bone from his side (God's a surgeon!), and into that weird chunk of flesh God breathes the life of Eve. She too comes from something that is not fully human (just part of one). Both Adam and Eve are created by God. They are individually crafted. They are made out of the same stuff. They are different, maybe even separate, and yet they are together, related to God, and dependent upon God for their existence.

The *Imago Dei:* The Image of God

So we know human beings are created by God, as individuals in community, and that to be human is to be related to and dependent upon God. But what is it about human beings that reflects the image of the God who created us? We have to remember that we reflect God's image because God is the one who established us in connection with God. There is no way that human beings can be separate from God. Given that we remember this, what does it mean to be human, in the image of God?

One of the most important things being created in the image of God means is that we are free. God freely chooses to create us and, in doing so, binds the divine self to the human. Because of our connection to and dependence on God, this means that freedom and relationship are inseparable in the *imago Dei*. Because being human means being two individuals together with God within the garden, being free has limits. God didn't give us independence (the ability to be individuals without others, with no need of others); God gave us freedom. In the book of Romans, we read that we are no longer to be slaves to sin, because of Christ's work. Instead, we are bound to God.

So freedom must mean something very different from simply "doing whatever I want to do." Freedom means that if your child is sick, you cancel your evening out and watch over her. Freedom means that if you are married, you resist the person who is flirting with you. Freedom means that if you are a hunter, you don't drive your SUV into a protected nature area. The Christian understanding of freedom means that even though you don't have to shovel your neighbor's walk in the winter, you do so anyway some-times. This understanding of freedom means that we are com-pletely free—*within limits*. In fact, it is these limits—other people, God, the rest of creation—which define our freedom. Freedom is not an abstract idea, and it's not a value. Freedom is something we live. It's something we do.

It is easy to conceive of freedom as being able to choose any possible option: We can have fries with that, choose vanilla over chocolate ice cream, opt for racing stripes, or pick up *To Kill a Mockingbird*. This is a part of freedom, because we're free to say "Yes, I'd like fries" or "No thanks." But to conceive of freedom only in terms of choice is to opt for a bland and limp understand-ing of freedom. Because to live freely, in Christian terms, is to live freely for others and for God. And being free for God and for oth-ers means, ironically, that our options are restricted.

So to say that freedom is limited is not negative—it means being free for God as God is free for us. And we are free for others, just as God is free for them. So we experience great joy when we give up a new dress so we can give our husband or boyfriend a new book, or when we spend all day slaving over a hot stove so our wife can have her chosen birthday meal. Or we're thrilled when our wife finally gets her book done—because loving her and wanting her to live out her calling meant doing more laundry and cleaning for a while.

In both stories in Genesis we read that God did not create human beings as isolated individuals, but as individuals together. To be human doesn't mean to be just one person, but a person connected to others. We are not just a collection of persons like a collection of rocks or coins. It's probably more like a connection of magnets: things bound together in a dynamic way, where elements are sep-arate but they affect one another. To be human is to be made out of the same stuff, to be created by God, and to be individuals together. So when God creates human beings in the image of God, we under-stand that by living with and for one another, we reflect God's free choice to be in relationship with us.

But this does not sound like freedom! After all, there are things we can't do. Is it freedom? In our own society in the United States, it is clear that even for the rugged individualist, freedom has limits. One cannot murder somebody without being punished for it. Likewise, a company cannot lie about its products. Our freedom lasts only so long as it doesn't hurt anyone else. We simply can't do whatever we want.

Even our freedom is created. Human beings simply do not have existence apart from God. Therefore, the image of God that human beings bear cannot be understood apart from God. Instead, the image of God which we reflect, we reflect because *God makes it happen*. We are not made out of the same substance as God. We are completely different from God because God is the Creator and we are creatures, but we reflect God's image because we are in free relationship with God as God has chosen to be in free relationship with us.

Christians also understand freedom as being total and genuine *within the limits of God and the neighbor*. This may not sound like freedom anymore. But it is, because within those limits we are completely free. It is just that our freedom, our choices, our decisions, our creativity aren't self-centered, for ourselves in spite of others, but are for the sake of others. What distinguishes the Christian concept of freedom is the assertion that these limits tell us what we are called to do, not what we don't have to do.

This is why Martin Luther took great pains to point out that freedom in Christ leads directly to the love of our neighbor. Luther understood the Ten Commandments as being much more than mere constraints on our actions: they aren't just a bunch of rules telling us what not to do. Martin Luther taught that "you shall not bear false witness" not only means we should not lie about (or to) our neighbor. It also means that we should speak the truth about others and protect their good names. We are not just to hold back from lying. We should also seek and preserve truth, the truth that our neighbor is created in the image of God! So that time in high school when I did not repeat the nasty gossip about my friend Jan, I was only partially obeying God. Because, you see, I did not actively stop the gossip or stand up for her in conversation. Had I done those things, I would have been truly free and demonstrated the freedom that is for God and for others. Freedom for Christians is *for* God and others, not freedom *from* God and others.

In fact, if to be in the image of God is to be connected to other people, then we are only free when we are in relationship with others. To be human means to be an individual, but not an individualist. Our uniqueness as individuals is created by God, but this does not mean that any one individual is more important or significant or like God than any other, nor does it mean that my connections to people don't matter. In fact, they are part of who I am. Individuals are important, but they are not supreme. We are individuals who belong together, who live in community, not individuals separate from other human relationships.

Interestingly, when we act freely, community is created. When we are free for others and for God, we build our connections with them. Freedom in the image of God actually builds relationships and community because it is freedom *for*. It's like growing a garden. If you're not me, that is. If you're me, you shove some dirt around, jam a seedling in it, soak it with the hose on put-out-the-fire strength, and then cross your fingers. To be a truly free gardener means that you work with what you've got for the sake of your garden. So you would carefully dig holes the right size. And the dirt you were digging in you would have enriched with compost (and all that other garden stuff I know is out there). And you would have given the plants the right gentle soaking. And you would have nurtured a garden, working with your soil and your plants, that grew into a fruitful enterprise. Putting yourself into the garden, with the particular plants and soil you have to work with— giving yourself—creates the garden (although many skilled gardeners tell me they cross their fingers, too).

Is the community more important than the individual? Or is the individual more important than the community? We need to make sure we avoid two misinterpretations. We need to avoid the tendency to make the individual more important than the community. In Philippians we are told to look not only to our own interests, but also to the interests of others. To say that "everyone is unique" is not to say that there's a competition for who's the best. We must remember that uniqueness means we are connected to others: We know we are unique because we know there are people who are different from us! Throughout Scripture we read of the importance of loving and serving others, because other human beings are also created and called by God. To be unique is not to live as ourselves despite other people, as sometimes happens when a person says, "I don't care what you think, this is just who I am—deal with it." Uniqueness should never be an excuse or a rationalization for treating others poorly.

In addition, throughout Scripture we read of the responsibilities we have for forming one another. In his letters collected in the Bible, the apostle Paul very specifically tells us that our use of our freedom has a major impact on those around us. So even though doing something (liking eating meat sacrificed to idols, which at the time was scandalous) may not harm our faith, it may cause a weaker brother or sister to stumble. It may be that two mature Christians could share a funny story about sex or wine or sarcasm—but they had best be cautious as they exert their freedom so that a person who struggles with his or her faith doesn't overhear this and assume that sex and wine and sarcasm are up for grabs. People tell sexist jokes, and then they're surprised when their sons think poorly of women, or their daughters think they have to have a man to be normal. Charles Barkley (a professional basketball player) said he wasn't a role model. But he is, whether he likes it or not, because people see him and learn from him.

When we live in community as human beings do, we have an impact on others around us, and they have an impact on us. We learn how to live from others around us. Children learn how to walk, talk, and love from those they are around as they grow up. Not only are we related to one another, but we form one another.

The other tendency we need to avoid is thinking that community is more important than individuals. Throughout Scripture we read that the individual is not supreme, but it's also clear that the community is not supreme. Individuals are precious to God, loved and known by God. After the woman of Samaria spoke with Jesus at the well, she rushed back to the city and proclaimed, "Come and see a man who told me everything I have ever done!" (John 4). Jesus knew the life of this woman, this particular, unique person. That we as individuals are precious to God and called as individuals (together!) is also sealed by the blessing of the Holy Spirit, who is our Comforter, Teacher, and Illuminator, the presence of God within us. The Holy Spirit dwells in the heart of each believer.

God is related to us as individuals within community. However, communities can be terrifying. Events like the Jamestown massacre and the deaths at Waco are burned in our minds as examples of what can happen when communities go horribly wrong. And Christian communities are certainly not exempt from the problem of destroying individuals in the name of the whole, declaring that this person or that person, or this group or that group, is inferior or unneeded. The apostle Paul reminds us of the error of this understanding in 1 Corinthians where he writes that "the lesser members of the body need all the more honor" (1 Cor. 12:23) because they are no less critical to the life of the body than other members. This harks back to the ancient declaration God makes to Abram in Genesis 12: *All* the families of the earth will be blessed through him.

God calls us as persons and as a people: we are individuals together. Being an individual is best understood as being distinct from others, meaning that there are others from whom we are distinct. But to say that we are like God because "we are relational" doesn't leave us with much insight as to what it means to be related as real, living and breathing human beings. What we also see in Genesis is that God loves the real, the actual, concrete, earthly person. We are really free to be who we are as individual human beings. This is the freedom to be an excellent street-sweeper, as Martin Luther King Jr. says, or an excellent teacher, an excellent cook, an excellent caregiver, a handsome man, an athletically gifted woman. This freedom, in other words, is not empty, not abstract. It is the freedom to be the way God has created us, for God and for others.

One of the implications of this understanding is good news to many people: Christians believe that human beings are created *to be human* and not to be God. God created us and put us in this earth, an earth which God called good and blessed. Our earthiness is part of our humanity, an integral part of who we are (and no more and no less fallen than the rest of us). We were created as body and spirit, not just spirits who have to have a body as a container, like hermit crabs who need to find discarded shells to live in. We are our bodies and our spirits together!

We are earthy! We were created as bodies, so we eat. We were created with bodies so we have skills, abilities. We were created with bodies so we have brains. We were created with bodies so our emotions are not separate from our bodily health and well-being. We are deaf people, and so we communicate with our fingers, hands, and arms. We are hearing so we speak and listen to music and conversation. Our lives are so interconnected that parts of our bodies become metaphors for our internal life, as when a blind person says, "I have a vision for the future of this law firm."

We have bodies, so we have pleasure. Pleasure in food, games, sex, work, sleep, cuddling, arm wrestling. We have pleasure in baseball, hot dogs, and apple pie. Or bocce, lime-and-ginger marinated chicken, and raspberry sorbet. Or hiking, Indian lentil dal, and fresh apricots. We take pleasure in one another, connect with one another when our separate bodies join in hugs, handshakes, a wiped tear, or a one-on-one game of pickup basketball. We have bodies so we walk the earthy ground, bathe in lake water, cuddle dogs, stroke cats, ride horses, pick flowers, gaze in amazement at the big sky of the plains, shiver in the frigid clear air of a mountaintop, walk content in a soft spring mist, swim with dolphins, or nurture a stunning wisteria onto the fence of our backyard.

This is why sex communicates so much about human experience *and* why sex is not necessary for people to be fully human. Sexuality expresses individuality together in magnificent ways. Sexuality is the pleasure and thrill of intimacy and promise, of enjoying the sheer delight of hormones and eroticism, of the binding of one human being to another. Sexuality is a magnificent expression of the way in which we are separate individuals with needs and desires that set us on fire and warm us, needs and desires that drive us to one another. Sexuality makes us keenly aware of our bodies and our earthiness whether we are in partnership with another or not.

But even though human beings are sexual beings (created with sexual organs, gendered, with some awareness of sexual feelings and drive) one does not have to have sex to be fully human. Surely, sexuality is a common human experience of the "self-acceptance through self-giving" that I mentioned in the last chapter, but it is not the only way. (And we can see that sometimes it is not the best way, for it is also within the expression of sexuality that the worst of human interaction can come about. I'll talk about this later.) Mother Teresa took vows of celibacy as a Catholic nun—meaning she vowed not to have sexual relationships. But she surely did live out in concrete, earthly, intimate, and physically connected ways what it means to accept one's self by giving of one's self. Sex is a gift of God, a wonderful gift like all God's gifts. It binds people together, gives them pleasure, and contributes greatly to the building of the community. There are other ways as well.

God created Adam and Eve with bodies, separate from one another, with one another, for one another. God placed Adam and Eve in a garden to enjoy its bounty and to care for it. Work, sex, eating, play, walking, gardening, all of these things are part of the story of the creation of human beings. So any discussion we have about being human must include this discussion of what it means to be people of the earth, people with bodies, bodies created by God. Our bodies are not bad. Like all else about being human they are created by God for God's glory, and even though humans sin, our bodies are inherently good, not a result of sin. This is why when C. S. Lewis writes of heaven in his book *The Great Divorce*, he describes heaven as a place where everything is so real, it hurts. The grass is so purely grass, so very real that the blades cut your feet—until you get used to the purity of this reality. And this is why when Lewis wrote of heaven in *The Last Battle* in *The Chronicles of Narnia*, heaven is just like earth, Narnia is exactly the same, only everything is healed, everything and everyone is living in peace and harmony, and all of Aslan's (Jesus') people are there with him, where they belong.

The image of the Peaceable Kingdom in Isaiah is just such an earthy and harmonious image, an existence of delight and security founded in the Messiah. In Isaiah 11 we read that not only will the poor and the meek be judged with fairness, but wolf and lamb, leopard and goat, lion and calf—all animals which would normally tear one another apart—will sleep quietly together, and a little child shall lead them. A toddler (and toddlers don't come from storks), we go on to read, will be able to play right on top of a snake's nest, because nothing shall destroy or hurt in all God's holy kingdom: "for the earth will be full of the knowledge of the LORD, as the waters cover the sea" (Isa. 11:9).

So Tuck, our little wonder puppy, will not destroy the bunny rabbit (not that Tuck is any good as a hunter—the bunny is safe). And Tuck won't have to be careful of moving vehicles. And Bosnians and Serbs will live in peace. And people of European heritage and people of African heritage will dwell in harmony. Women and men, doctors and nurses, CEO's and assembly-line workers will live in harmony with teachers and the homeless—and the homeless will have a place. The knowledge of God will fill creation and all will be well. Life will be full and abundant and at peace—like when we take a walk with our dog in the soft sunshine and meet up with others who are equally at peace walking the earth. Life will be full and bellies will be full and crops will grow and trees will shade and water will flow—righteousness like a river, and justice like an ever-flowing stream.

We are wrong when we think the life of redemption is otherworldly and abstract. It is real and tangible and imaginable. Christ's incarnation is a declaration of affirmation of human, earthly, life-in-the-world. Jesus affirmed celebration and affirmed human existence. So the life of the Peaceable Kingdom is life lived concretely with and for God, ourselves, and others, in delight and justice and peace.

And because we must always remember that this Peaceable Kingdom is *God's* good work, we must be careful to avoid the error of thinking our version of earthly life is one we are entitled to simply because we are created in the image of God. We can lose ourselves in the joy, power, and freedom of human existence, and pretty soon God is out at the margins of existence. Believing we can be *like* God *without* God leads us in some dangerous directions. Thinking about the *imago* as a possession has led human beings to think that they own the earth and all therein. We are little gods. The world is ours and we can do whatever we want with it! It is a small wonder that with our consumer culture and our sin we would assume that dominion means the world is ours, and that God is Lord over all—except what we have and want!

The argument runs like this. If we assume that the *imago Dei* is something *we* have, then we think it belongs to us. So when we read in Genesis that God gave Adam and Eve dominion over all the earth, we say that the earth is ours to do with as we please. When we say that being human is something we *have*—we "own" it— then we are saying that we are human *apart from God.*

The problem here is that dominion doesn't mean ownership—it means stewardship. Because of our sin and confusion with the image of God (and other things), we find ourselves with a whole host of problems. Partially because we Christians have traditionally held that mind and freedom are so important to being human, we have become people who think that technology—any technology— is good just because we can invent it. In fact, science has become almost a hallmark of correct thinking in our society, even though science and technology have produced guns, bombs, chemical weapons, tools of execution, and methods of extinction. We think technology is good, and invention equals progress, so we produce more and more vehicles that pollute our planet, and overuse (and abuse) our finite resources (recent estimates say we will run out of oil within seventy to eighty years). Our desire for timber has destroyed rain forests (and along with them thousands of species, some of which could save human life), woodlands, and wetlands and led to problems with erosion.

These are just a couple of examples of problems with our use of technology, because of the way we use our minds and freedom. But use of technology isn't the only problem, and, of course, much of technology has been a blessing to creation. The way we use our minds and freedom has led us down other destructive paths: Our use of our minds and freedom has led Christians in the past to say that blacks are inferior and that women are irrational. It has led some of us to say that all Jews are cheap and all Native Americans are lazy drunks. When we human beings have the opportunity to use our minds and freedom the way we want, we tend to use them in *our* favor. We tend to look to our own interests, and not the interests of others.

Which is why we have to take seriously the difficulty of defin- ing any *one* thing as what it means to be created in the image of God. Our minds certainly are important to being human: Thinking can produce wisdom, practical advice, technology that nurtures and prospers human life, and sophisticated agriculture that benefits humans and the earth, among many other things. And freedom is important to being human, too; especially in our country we cringe when we see individuality stifled simply because a person doesn't conform to the dominant culture, and we're glad to live in a country where freedom of expression is valued.

But we need to remember that these freedoms are way more limited for some than for others, and that the thinking of some people is held to be way more valuable than the thinking of others. An example of this that drives so many people around the bend is standardized testing. Some high schoolers and college students do quite well on these tests, and sometimes because they are quite intelligent. However, some people do quite well because they take tests well. And we Christians need to be careful of assuming that scales of intelligence measure how human we are! Mostly, what we have to remember is that human thinking and human freedom can never be something we *have*.

One of the things I grew up with in my house was artificial implants, since Dad designed them. There were always a few strewn around Dad's study downstairs, and every once in a long while, some of the plastic versions would show up. It's not something we would talk about every day, but every once in a while, we could stop and take notice and Dad would explain how the knee worked and how the hip is a ball and socket joint that rotates inside a cup. Dad always explores ideas out loud: It became a family joke eventually, after Dad had repeatedly asked us at the dinner table if we understood how the walls were being put together in the building that was going up next to his. (They were concrete panels that were put together using pins set in one another . . . I think.) And on Tuesdays we would have a special dessert and a Bible study after dinner.

It was a shock to me when I got to the Christian college I attended and found that there were students who were appalled that Christians actually thought about evolution. To them it was a sacrilege. To me the conflict was confusing. My Dad was devout, and not only believed in God but followed God. He believed in the authority of the Bible and he was a scientist. What I became aware of was the many ways that religion claims to be science and that science makes religious claims—or tries to obviate religion. Could the debate be resolved? Was the Bible reduced to spiritual mush while science offered real knowledge? Or does science, like religion, often exceed its own bounds?

I discovered that part of our differences lay in how people understand God to be the Creator. For many scientists who are Christians, science is a way of getting to know the world in which we live, the bodies in which we live, and various ways of coping with this world. Science helps us discover and understand what God has created. Of course, science can be a method of control to some people, and some fall victim to the illusion that science gives us real, Creator-like power.

But it doesn't. When Christians affirm that God is the Creator, we affirm that this world is dependent on God and we affirm that God calls us to know this world. Indeed, the command of God to Adam and Eve to subdue the earth inside the garden and till it out-side the garden assumes that we can work in harmony with the cre-ation. Throughout the Bible we find references to using our minds wisely, developing wisdom, the delight in creation, the use of tools. The words in Proverbs remind us of the nature of our knowledge. It is real, but it is limited. We are not to *rely* on our own under-standing. The knowledge of all that is is God's alone. Affirming that God is the Creator is affirming that God is the source of all that is.

Humans, in the *Imago Dei*

We need to gather up all these thoughts. What does all this mean? What basic things can we say about being human?

We can say that to be created in the image of God means that human beings are diverse. The image of God is seen in diversity and difference and uniqueness, not sameness or identity. We are not all required to be perfectly rational or have the same perfectly obe-dient will to reflect the image of God. Because human beings are created in the image of God as individuals together, every one of us will think differently and be set different tasks by God. We all have different talents, different levels of intelligence, different desires and goals. And we'll walk and talk and look different from one another. Your third-grade teacher and Albert Einstein. The nicest kid in school and the meanest. Chris Roc and Bill Cosby and Vanilla Ice and Queen Latifah and Rosie O'Donnell and Chow Yun Fat and the United States president and Mother Teresa. And the little girl born in China this very second and the little boy being born in Kenya right now. Those in our midst whose mental abilities are in a world of their own are made in the image of God just like us. Carpenters, vegetarians, ranchers, Greenpeace workers, and NRA policy makers, in all their diversity are made in the image of God.

No matter who you are reading this book right now, you are created in the image of God. *Right now*. The person that you are right now reflects the image of God. You may be a geek in high school. You are created in the image of God. You may be mentally ill. You are created in the image of God. You may be the most popular boy or girl in your class. You are created in the image of God. You may have just sinned or been sinned against. You are created in the image of God. You may be physically disabled. You are created in the image of God. You may be a convict just let out of prison. You are created in the image of God. You may have just had an affair and cheated on your husband or wife. You are created in the image of God. Your husband or wife may have cheated on you. You are created in the image of God.

What is significant here is that the image of God is reflected not only in the content of this difference, but also in the existence of difference. It is not that we all add up together like a mathematical equation to equal the image of God $(1 + 1 = 2)$, but the image of God is reflected in the relationships that are set between us. Our differences are as vast as is the entire human race—past, present, and future.

And this is why we can also say that the image of God is seen partially in us individually, fully in the community. This is what I referred to at the beginning of the chapter as Christian maturity. Full humanity means full community because human beings are created as individuals together, free for God and others. We cannot talk about the image of God as existing completely in just one particular human being, even if we talk about a particular person as representative of all human beings. We are only able to see the image of God because of Christ as God *for all human beings*. It is Christ who restores the image of God.

This is why the apostle Paul refers to us as the body of Christ. To be fully human does not mean to be really good specimens of Homo sapiens. To be human is not to be adult. It is not to be perfect. It is not to be mature. Any concept we have of the community being defined in terms of perfection or adulthood goes out the window.

Does this mean we reject maturity? No. Maturity is defined in a way much different from being adult. Which is a good thing, because many of us are adults, but are not mature (take for instance, the mutation that occurs in my husband when he watches University of Michigan football every fall, or my own obsession with cartoons). Christian maturity includes all members of the body of Christ, and to be mature means *by definition* that our maturity is linked to others. We cannot be mature on our own: *we cannot be fully human on our own.*

So full humanity in the Christian sense *includes* adults and teenagers, convicts and ex-convicts, tall and short, law-abiders and holier-than-thou's, the sophisticated and the oafish, for all have sinned and fall short of the glory of God, and all are forgiven. Christian maturity refers to the fullness of being human, which by definition refers to the fullness of being human together.

So What Is a Person?

To be human means one is created and called in the image of God. To be fully human doesn't necessarily mean to be mature. Nor does it mean to be self-actualized. Our society is such that as a people we have done much and continue to do much that makes people feel horrible about themselves, and we do this in the church no less than outside it. Christians take this problem seriously, for Christians affirm the significance of the individual both to God and to the people God has created and called. But self-esteem in Christian terms directs us to understand ourselves as connected to God. The self-esteem that the *imago Dei* offers is the esteem of a self that is *called, belongs*, and *serves*. Christians understand that the human being, the self, is not alone, that it cooperates and celebrates with others, and finds its own good and fulfillment—joy, generosity, and calling—in the good of the other person.

3

Conflict, Sin, and Grace

Conflict

*C*onflict is both creative and dangerous. I must say that one of my favorite discoveries of seminary study was that conflict is not necessarily bad. Some who know me will say that I believe this because I kind of enjoy a bit of conflict now and then. They'll say it's the Basque in me—what one person referred to as my "terrorist instinct" and what I prefer to call "strong feeling." Whatever the reason, to say that conflict isn't necessarily sin is not to say that conflict should be the order of the day, but that individuals striving together toward good should expect this. To say that there is some goodness in conflict is to say that individuals are important within community.

How does conflict help reflect individuality in a good way? Have you ever had a tug of wills with a young child—and the child turned out to be *right?* It is often a general pattern that parents and caregivers find themselves in again and again. They explain how something is going to go, but the child says, "Wait! Let me explain." Reluctantly the older person listens, and discovers to his or her chagrin that the child has a valid point. At my sister's old house they had a side door and a back door, and the side door would be open, but the back door (where the doorbell was) would be locked. The kids knew that they were supposed to walk around the house to the side door to come back inside. So on that very snowy, cold day, four-year-old Isaac rang the doorbell. And rang the doorbell again. And rang. And rang, and rang, and rang. Finally, my sister, losing her patience and angry at Isaac for doing what he wasn't supposed to do, went to the door, prepared for a speech, only to find that Isaac's gloves—the kind that get strung through the coat sleeves—were stuck in the door that locked. He was attached, and the only thing he could do was ring. And he kept on ringing until help came.

Of course the conflict here is more a parent's perceived conflict with the child than an actual confrontation between parent and child. But there are similarities: Anytime someone is doing something differently than we wish or differently than we suggested, we feel conflict. That other person is asserting his or her individuality in such a distinct way that it conflicts with mine. Resolving that conflict, like opening the door and unsticking the gloves, solves a problem.

It sure sounds nice to say that Christians believe the good of all is found in the good of each, and it's wonderful to think of human fulfillment in terms of the health and welfare of each individual comprising the community. This is why we can also say that to be created in the image of God means that we will have conflict. Our differences are vast, rich and fruitful, and marvelous, but our differences don't exist for their own sake. It's not enough just to be "different." This difference, insofar as we are free to be different, is *for* God and *for* the other. So conflict is inherent in the image of God, and is not a result of sin (although there is conflict that is sinful, just as there is uniqueness that is sinful). We are individuals with individual wills.

It makes sense that conflict should arise since we reflect the image of God in our individuality in community. But conflict reflects different perspectives just as much as it reflects plain stubbornness (much of which, except for *my* stubbornness, probably falls under the category of sinful stubbornness). If we take conflict seriously, especially within our Christian communities, as the body of Christ seeking to do God's will, then we can see that this conflict of wills leads toward life, precisely the life of the community. This is a tricky concept, because our everyday understanding of conflict connotes problems of hierarchy and domination, selfishness, pettiness, even incompetence. However, in its grounding in the doctrine of the *imago Dei* conflict requires merely that we work things out, and that human community, because we are individuals, requires being worked out. Not only that, but the whole purpose of creating each human being individually and uniquely is precisely for cooperation. We need one another precisely so we *can* work together.

But then the realtor takes the elderly woman for a couple hundred thousand, your child can't resist the urge to clock her brother upside the head with a hammer, or you say something cruel—intending to or not—to one of your friends. Things go wrong. Conflict which can help us figure things out, do better, and solve problems becomes something we turn on ourselves, others, and God.

People egg each other on and sometimes seek conflict. At meetings of religion professors it has become trendy to observe that the best teaching method is to make the classroom a dangerous place for students. The thought is that this is what prompts growth. Some teachers say that the best thing they can do for their students is to break down everything they know and build it back up again. If we aim for conflict, that's what we're going to get, and when conflict is the goal, people are not our top concern. Conflict is not a reality we should work toward bringing to fruition in our lives. Love, on the other hand, is something we want to aim toward, for it puts God and others at the forefront of our minds. Conflict is something we should neither avoid nor aim toward—it's simply a fact of life. It's not necessarily a bad part of life, it simply means there is struggle in life.

Conflict is a puzzling phenomenon. Without it, people would never be able to grow and learn. Without conflict husbands and wives would never discover the depth of their love for one another, or the depth of the human being that they are bound with for life, since the struggles between those who call each other "beloved" force us to see one another from a new perspective. Without conflict—disagreement, frustration, stubbornness—would my husband and I have learned that we both love order and organization, just in different ways? Our very identities are formed partially through conflict as we begin to understand ourselves as different from our parents with wills and minds and ideas of our own.

Conflict in the workplace can be the birth of new and creative ideas. When scientists argue back and forth on the best way to do an experiment, often a better way emerges from their conflict. Making mistakes and trying again can lead to the right solution. In churches we often see conflicts over how things should be done. Many of us tend to understand these disagreements ("they never do the coffee right") by assuming the other person just doesn't get it. Are others really that wrongheaded? Or is it really a situation in which people are able to pool their different perspectives, get a better picture of their community vision or project, and formulate a more constructive approach?

But you'll notice that my language here is guarded. We can see that conflict between individuals can help to solve problems, accomplish projects, and create community, but it can easily go around the bend and turn into self-serving, self-effacing, other-abusing, relationship-harming dynamics. Conflict is a helpful way for us to talk not only about individuality-in-community but about sin. The two are closely related. Conflict can be blessed and healed by Jesus Christ, who restores what we call conflict to its proper place, the work of God in God's diverse creation.

There is conflict with the circumstances of life. A friend and I were discussing not too long ago the tremendous paperwork that adulthood involves these days. Mortgages, bills, tax materials, the sheer volume of mail, junk and otherwise. Everyone produces paper, now that we have those handy dandy computers to help put it out, and we need help in interpreting it and organizing it. There are medical bills, all sorts of utilities, phone offers, etc., etc., etc. We used to dream when we were children that we couldn't wait to be grown-ups because then we could do what we wanted.

Ha.

Adulthood is much more complicated than that, and much more full of responsibility. And while we were right, thank goodness, that these are our lives to live, we were (blissfully) unaware of how hard life is when we bear responsibilities. And this isn't just because we have responsibility, but because we bear responsibility in the face of circumstances beyond our control. Pursuing our lives, our gifts, our Christian joy in the midst of a world we do not control makes Christian life a constant adventure.

If we could control circumstances, our babies would not be still-born, or come into the world with genetic abnormalities that make their lives difficult at best and short at worst. If we could control circumstances, spouses would not betray us, and those we fall in love with would fall in love with us. If we could control circumstances, our loved ones would not be alcoholic, our cars would not break down when we can't afford to fix them, our jobs would not be cut, children would not suffer and go unloved and unnurtured, the job market would not fail us, police would watch *our* neighborhoods too, people would not be destroyed over religious beliefs, our families would not say hurtful things, classrooms would see the intelligence in all students, and people would not be put down. Most of us, if we could control the world, would not want to make it so much less exciting and variable as we would want to eliminate the ability of circumstances to hurt and destroy and sadden.

But we cannot control circumstances. In the Garden of Gethsemane Jesus Christ himself knelt down and prayed that God would take this cup from him. According to the Gospel accounts, Christ had already foretold that he would be crucified, but even so the horror became overwhelming. At the same time, he knew he wanted to do God's will. He was being persecuted. He knew with certainty that that sort of persecution has only one possible end. By committing himself to that way of being in the world, he became unsafe, insecure. A friend described parenthood to me in a similar way: As soon as you become pregnant, she said, you are no longer safe. You, your heart and soul, are always at risk.

Being at risk gives us an inkling of God's own heart and passion. For as soon as God's Only Begotten became human in this world, Jesus was in the midst of circumstances. Jesus Christ didn't just put up with people making fun of him. Jesus had to put up with thorns, but far worse than when you cut yourself pruning your rosebushes or putting a stem in a vase, Jesus had to put up with a whole crown of thorns, jammed onto his head. Nails in his feet and hands, a slow death.

Conflict is not just between persons. We also have conflict with God. This is something Jesus himself had to struggle with in his own experience of suffering and grief. Jesus Christ makes it clear, as the one who is fully divine and fully human and full person of the Trinity, that to talk about circumstances as though they are separate from God's strength and power and love is false. How God exists in the midst of our life circumstances may be a mystery or hard truth, as it was for Jesus Christ in the garden. He did not want to taste the cruel cup of suffering unto death. But if it was the one that God passed to him, then Jesus said, "Thy will be done." Jesus himself admitted God's presence in the circumstances. As God's own self-revelation Jesus Christ exemplifies for us life in the midst of all life, whatever it may be, life dependent upon God.

In the play *J.B.*, Archibald MacLeish retells the story of Job. J.B. asserts from the beginning that God is good. But MacLeish offers an interesting theological twist. At the end, after all the destruction J.B. suffers, the heartache, the illness, the abandonment by his wife, his contention with God is resolved not because God wins by force of argument, but because J.B. chooses to accept God. In the words of the play, God is forgiven by J.B. It is J.B.'s choice that resolves the situation.

We Christians aren't used to considering wrestling with God an acceptable approach to the Divine. But Jews are. In the play *Angels in America*, an AIDS patient visited by an oppressive angel is told to wrestle with the angel and demand a blessing before sending it on its way, just like Jacob, because it is the Jewish way. It is the Jewish way to converse and argue with God, not, certainly not, because God is manipulable, but because God is real and active and very present. So Jesus' conversation with God in the Garden is not some errant part of the story that doesn't quite fit in. And while Mary, the mother of Jesus, doesn't actually contend with God, she does, indeed, converse with the Divine. "How can this be?" she asks. In the midst of circumstances beyond her control, Mary chooses to cooperate with God for good reasons. She doesn't just sigh and shrug her shoulders in passive resignation. Conflict with God is real, and because it is conflict with God, it goes to the core of our lives, making our lives all the more vivid and real, both in pain and in joy.

Finally, conflict in community has the potential of real fruitfulness. Individuals strive forward together toward God's will for the world. In fact, it is critical that Christians take individuality seriously, for without it the body withers. The trick is to get that individuality in organic, healthy working order so that each individual has her own God-designed place for her own sake and the sake of the body.

But conflict without love, and without that striving for the work of God in the world, can lead only toward destruction. We must remember that when we are in conflict, with God, ourselves, or others, we can fall into the trap of taking our conflict and hitting others over the head with it. Instead of striving, we turn conflict into strife. We can destroy community with conflict by abusing our freedom. Instead of being free for the other and free for the calling to which we have been called, we act as though we are free from the responsibility of the hard work of compromise and cooperation, and free from the responsibility of the results of our actions. Because conflict can lead to good does not mean it always leads to good and we should look for ways to create it.

And here is where we see the danger zone. Conflict can help us understand an aspect of sin, since it gives us a sense of alienation and antagonism between God, ourselves, and others. Remember that sin is a derangement of our nature as God created it. When we seek conflict for its own sake, we seek danger and risk and we even try to create it, like when we say something mean or harsh just to provoke a sibling, friend, or colleague. But when we do that, we derange goodness. We take what God has arranged well, and we mess it up. We take what God has put together and we put it asunder. When we seek conflict, we reject freedom. Instead of being *for* God, ourselves, and others, we are against them.

For All Have Sinned and Fall
Short of the Glory of God

All this talk about freedom and conflict, even when it is freedom *for* God and *for* others, leaves us with a slightly uneasy feeling in our stomach. Not because we're worried about our own freedom, but because when we talk about freedom in the Christian life, we immediately admit that we can't control other people's actions. We worry about how they will handle their freedom and whether they will do it properly. And while many of us don't worry about our own freedom, we generally (not all of us) live within a system that is anti-freedom because the freedom we are called to is too unknown.

Freedom takes us to places that we fear. We fear because we have to give up control when we live in freedom with Christ. This is the irony of Christian freedom. We also fear because Christian freedom takes away our favorite definition of sin: a list of rights and wrongs which each of us has, a list that regulates and defines which behaviors are acceptable and which are not. People should not wear jeans to church. The right word in the Lord's Prayer is "trespasses," not "debts." Women should not work outside the home. People of different races shouldn't marry. Christians should not horde money.

How should we understand the limits of our freedom? If the limit of our freedom is God and each other (and we should also add the earth and all its stuff, since this also belongs to God apart from us), what is sin? Do we destroy being human by sinning?

Does sinning matter in any way? The answer to this question is a thundering "Yes!" But not for the reasons we generally imagine. Sin is not a list kept of rights and wrongs. Nor is sin something that irretrievably cuts us off from God. Sin matters, not because it shows all our misbehavior, but because it separates us from God, and keeps us from knowing, enjoying, and glorifying God. Sin matters because it deranges our nature, ruins what it means to be human beings created in the image of God. Sin matters because it destroys freedom—we refuse to be who we are because we refuse to acknowledge the limits or structure of what it means to be human. We try to *be* God, instead of living *with* God at our center.

Sin breaks our communities. In a recent book on sin, Cornelius Plantinga points out that sin is like pollution: To something that is good and beautiful, sin adds elements that ruin that good thing. And by adding elements that ruin goodness, sin breaks up what exists as good. So when a marriage partner has an affair, the marriage relationship is polluted, and the relationship is broken down.

If that marriage is to stay together, an enormous amount of forgiveness, reconciliation, and difficult work is needed to restore and clean what has been broken and tainted. Sin is first and foremost against God, but sin also infects the rest of our lives.

But one of the concerns many people have about sin is seen in an assumption: that sin eliminates our reflection of the image of God. We think, perhaps, that if we have sinned, then the image of God is destroyed. And if this is the case, then our existence as human beings is worthless, repulsive, and disgusting, not only to God, but by extension also to other human beings. And in our arrogance, we look at others and assume that the *imago Dei* has been erased in them. We tend to make allowances for the rough treatment of prisoners because of the horrific crimes they have committed, and we tend to think that child abusers are less than or other than human, even using the phrase "that's not human" to describe their behavior.

The problem is that it is human. We make allowances for some crimes and decry others. We call rapists less than human, but we think of corporate raiders as operating within the system, and corporate executives who profit—enormously—off the sweat of third-world workers as smart businesspeople. Is that more human? Sin is all the same in the end—an affront against God.

But sin never destroys what is human about us. If we affirm that to be human is to be created by God, held by God in relationship with God, then there is nothing we can do to eliminate what it means to be human. It is not our effort or abilities or characteristics that make us human, but God's own will. And if we take careful note of the Genesis passages, we see that what sin does is remove us from God's presence, and sin leads to a life of more sin. But it does not eliminate what it means to be human. It does not destroy the image of God in which we have been created.

The Importance of Sin

So sin doesn't destroy what it means to be created in the image of God. It doesn't destroy what is fundamentally human. If this is the case, then is sin still a useful concept? Does it still matter? The answer to this is yes, for sin taints and destroys our knowledge and love of God and each other, it makes the life of creatures' *imago Dei* confusing and difficult and heinous at times. Sin removes us from fellowship with God, which is the core of what it means to be human. Sin and the *imago Dei* coexist.

So what does sin affect? *Why* does it still matter? Because our sins and our sinfulness taint our relationship with God and others. We do not become more fully human simply by not sinning. Likewise, we can't nurture a relationship with God simply by rigidly following the Ten Commandments. This is because the Ten Commandments—and the great commandment to love the Lord our God with all our heart, soul, strength, and mind and our neighbor as ourselves—aren't rules separate from God, but laws from God for life with God and others. The right way to follow the Ten Commandments is not to obey them, but to obey *God* by following them. Sin matters because it affects our relationship with God. Sin does not have a life of its own—it ruins the good that exists.

What Is Sin?

How does sin affect what it means to be a person? Clearly, it does not mean we cease to be human. Sin does not change the fact that God loves us and sustains us, nor does sin change the fact that God loves and sustains the other person. Calvin said that no matter how incompetent, lazy, or stupid some people are, they are still creatures in the image of God and we should look at them that way.

But as Christians we must also remember that our created purpose and drive is for God, not against God. Sin sets us back in this growth, drives us away; sin kills our roots. Sin affects our entire person, causing us anxiety, killing our character, turning virtue into vice. One sin leads to others and makes it easier to sin. Our sin leads others around us toward sin and sinfulness. Sin ultimately affects us in such a way that we long to be our own god, we long to be our own Creator, and we shove God out of the center, and put ourselves in God's rightful place.

Do you remember the conversation between Eve and the serpent in Genesis? Adam and Eve are out walking around the garden and the serpent engages Eve. The serpent asks her if God really meant what he said about the tree of the knowledge of good and evil. When Eve replies, the first theological conversation begins. The conversation is not *with* God. Rather, Eve and the serpent talk *about* God as though God could not hear them! The serpent gets Eve to think and ponder and pass judgment on what God really meant when God gave the commandment. She assumes she knows what God is thinking.

We do this all the time: We assume we know what the other person is thinking, and we act on our assumptions and rationalize some sort of control over the situation or the relationship. Dietrich Bonhoeffer, in *The Cost of Discipleship*, tells a story every parent or guardian can relate to. There, you see, a child's father calls him and says, "It's time to get ready and go to bed." And the child starts thinking, "Hmm . . . Dad really wants me to make sure I'm rested. But I know that if I go out and play for a couple of hours, I'll get really tired, and then I'll sleep much better. So when Dad said 'Go to bed' he really meant 'Go out and play for a couple of hours.' "

Sin turns us into class-A rationalizers. Eve's conversation with the serpent was a conversation in which she rationalized about what God *really* meant, which results in an action directly contrary to what God specifically said. Adam is with her, the text tells us, yet does nothing throughout this, and takes the fruit when it is offered. Both have sinned, and both fall short of the glory of God.

We should make a couple of notes about this story. We should not say that they never should have had this conversation; after all, God created humans to think for themselves. God does not want blind robots who wouldn't question God. The problem with this conversation was that it was *about* God, not *with* God. God was cut out of the picture entirely. Adam and Eve acted as though God wasn't the center of their existence, the center of their being, the very foundation of what it meant to be them. God was not a factor at all.

Second, Adam is no dupe in this game. Eve did not make Adam fall. Both are equally to blame. If you want to twist texts, then remember that only Adam receives the command of God not to eat of the tree of the knowledge of good and evil. But let's not twist the text. They both disobey; perhaps in different ways, but they both fall short. And now, because they push God out of the middle, because they want God's position, they are no longer going to live with justice between themselves. The Garden of Eden ain't big enough for the both of 'em.

In sin God is no longer the orienting point of life. And this is ultimately unrewarding and unfulfilling. Recently I asked a pastor friend of mine about vocational concerns. He said the key to understanding our "calling" is that our lives are not our own. Even though my life is *my* life, and only I can live it, it cannot be without recognizing that it belongs to God. An airplane cannot be what it was designed to be unless it is flying and being flown by a pilot. Without God at our center, we are not ourselves, not what we should be, not living out the purpose for which God intended us. Sin is actions and attitudes which ruin us, ruin other people, and ruin our relationship with and response to God. The fall of Adam and Eve was not the entrance of something new apart from God, but the way in which Adam and Eve, both responsible for their actions, abandoned God and removed God from the rightful place in the center of the garden. They removed themselves from God's presence. Individually and together they destroyed what was good. Then, when God called to them and was with them, they became aware of their own sin.

In the terms which we used in the last chapter, freedom *for* God and *for* others, sin is freedom *against* God and *against* others— freedom in spite of God and others. Sin is claiming any right that gains us something while hurting someone else. Sin is throwing our individuality in someone's face or reducing another person to a representative of a philosophy or opinion ("You're such a Republican," "You're such a Democrat"). Sin is claiming our freedom while not fighting for the freedom of others. We sin when we reject the freedom God has called us to.

There are two surprising problems in Christian freedom which require an addition to our typical understanding of freedom. When we talk about freedom *for* God and others, we are talking about responsibility. We respond to others and to God, in freedom, but we do so as people connected to God and to others. Therefore, we must be vigilant of our freedom lest we turn it into either abuse of the other or abuse of ourselves.

When we take our responsibilities to God and others seriously, we sometimes go wrong. Responsibility, like all other things in life, requires balance. This is not a balance between doing good for the other and not doing good for the other, but a finely adjusted sense of what it means to be loving toward God, self, and other in a particular situation. So when I consider my responsibility to another person, I need to remember not to dominate him or her. This is the abuse of the other person. Other people are not our duties. We may have duties toward them, but we should not treat them as a task on our "to do" list. So when one of my high school friends had sex, and I was shocked, it became my duty to make sure she understood how wrong she was. What I did was twist the command to love my neighbor. Instead of following the command to be loving, I made it my responsibility for her to obey commands. Calvin has a pithy observation about this human tendency: he wants us "not to inquire about another's duties, but every man should keep in mind that one duty which is his own." And Jesus reminds us in the Sermon on the Mount to worry about the log in our own eye before we worry about the speck of dust in our neighbor's eye.

The problem of turning people into a duty is twofold. First, it treats the other person like a thing instead of a person. Romantic partners, coworkers, parents, ministers, medical personnel—everyone has to deal with the temptation of this abuse. It is generally not an abuse born out of ill will but rather out of passionate or stalwart conviction in the right way to do things. It is fundamental mistreatment of another person as a thing. Second, because it treats the other person as a thing, this abusive action assumes that God is clueless and is not working through that other person. Sin, and especially our sinful self-deception, allows us to think that the sinfulness of other people clouds *their* understanding, but not our own. *We are not God.* Only God knows what God is calling that other person to, and how the Spirit is working through him or her.

The second problem is the flip side of the abuse of the other: the abuse of the self. In the church, "service to God" can even be part of the problem. A mother could take caring for children so seriously that all her other responsibilities are neglected. She neglects her other gifts, her husband, other relationships, herself. In providing for his family, a father might take his work to such extremes that it pushes responsibilities to wife and children and God's creation right to the margins and out of the picture. Sometimes we see obligations as totally compelling. We see each duty as a binding law, completely binding, each in its own right.

Does this mean that parents should not take their children seriously? Absolutely not! A parent's children have responsibilities of their own, to their gifts, and calls, and relationships, and this freedom of the individual child in community must be nurtured for its own sake. These abuses arise because we allow one thing to be the limit of our lives, and that one thing is not God who binds us to others and ourselves.

So We're Sinful. Now What?

How do we know what our responsibilities are? How do we know what our sins are? One of the main catalysts for the Reformation came down to this very question. Martin Luther was an obsessed monk, obsessed with his sin. Sometimes he would be in the confessional for hours on end, driving his superiors nuts as he doggedly went through each sin he could remember. He couldn't bear to leave a single sin out because an unconfessed sin would go unatoned and he would be unsaved.

His superiors sent him to study the New Testament (a novel way to get someone to lighten up) and Martin Luther faced grace. He had come to the realization that he would never be able to remember all his sins, and he would never be able to identify them. And that was the point: Christ came for sinners, for people like Martin

Luther, and people like me, who sin all the time, live sinfully, and cannot extricate ourselves. And the salvation and forgiveness of Jesus Christ is not a listing of which acts are wiped away, but a complete restoration of the person to God, which is accomplished for us *without our work*. We need to know our sinful selves so that we can grow in this restored relationship as justified selves. We are simultaneously without sin and sinful, and we are always being reconciled to God.

Grace and Forgiveness

The forgiveness of our sins is the grace of God, a grace that is costly, not cheap. Cheap grace is when we ease our consciences and give ourselves permission to do whatever we want. This would be our rationalization right before we gossip: We roll our eyes at ourselves and maybe mutter something like "Christians aren't perfect, just forgiven" as some sort of excuse for what we are about to do. Or we follow our own drives and say right up front, "I'm fallen," "I'm only human," even if these drives lead us into a sinful sexual relationship because "it's one of my needs."

So we admit that sin doesn't change the fact that we are created in the image of God. Does that mean that we should sin so that we can receive the grace of God again and again? "By no means!" the apostle Paul tells us (Rom. 6:2), for this behavior has nothing to do with true grace. This is cheap grace, a disguise for the rejection of God. It is not unlike the rejection of his father by the prodigal son. Jesus told the story about a father who had two sons who knew they would get a large inheritance from their father. The younger son said, "Give it to me now!" and off he went, spending the money like there was no tomorrow. The prodigal son took his inheritance (grace) and said, "Forget you" and ran off, abandoning his father and the love his father gave him so freely. (I may have done this once or twice as a teenager myself!)

Costly grace is the return of the prodigal son. This grace is costly both to the son and to the father. The son had spent everything he had and was reduced to living in pigsties, eating what pigs left behind. Knowing he had nothing, that he had betrayed his father's gift and was worthless and not to be considered, he threw himself on his father's mercy, the only mercy he knew. This costs us control of our lives and requires that we give our lives up. (To save our lives we must lose them.) I heard one person say that this should really be the parable of the prodigal father. Prodigal doesn't just mean wasteful, as in the son's waste of his inheritance. It also means lavish, as in the love the father poured out in welcoming home his wasteful son.

Here, authentic and costly grace is seen in the abandoned and rejected father's open embrace and outpouring love to restore the relationship with his beloved child. Costly grace is the restoration of the real relationship, not merely eliminating the wrong. Costly grace is when the parent of a teenager doesn't just say "I'll pay for the damage to the car" but also holds her child and assures her it won't be held against her. Costly grace is one spouse not just staying married after an affair but working to heal the marriage. Costly grace isn't just amnesty for sins of political oppression, but confession and a change in life that indicates oppression won't be repeated and the new life will be one of reconciliation.

The cheap version of the *imago Dei* is living any way one likes, despite God, despite others. It is living as though the *imago Dei* is something we have, that belongs to us, like a book or a bottle of wine that we can do whatever we want with. The costly version of the *imago Dei* is life with God and others, *for* God and others, recognizing that our lives are not our private property. Our lives are God's. If we want to know and love God and others, and if we want to be known and loved, our lives are costly. But it costs God as well. And that is why sin matters.

Forgiveness

If I am called by God, and have been forgiven and restored, I recognize that I am not God. When we accept forgiveness from God, we realize that we are all equal before the Almighty. No human being has the position or right to pass judgment on you, no

matter what stupid or mean thing you did when you were young—
or no matter what you did last week. They are not God—they cannot condemn you. It may be that your parents had to discipline you,
or someone else turned their back on you, but this does not mean
that you were, or are, condemned. Nor can we play God in anyone
else's life, deciding whether they are condemned or forgiven,
asserting that a person who would do or believe such a thing is
damned. Only Christ can condemn, our Scriptures say, and Christ
did not come to condemn the world, but to save it. We cannot
condemn.

When it comes to an actual situation, though, it's hard to forgive. We often don't feel willing or peaceful or generous. It's hard.
In fact, forgiveness is also partly defined by just how hard it is. It
is hard—very, very hard. It is so hard that we Christians find ourselves saying the most ironic things. In a conversation I had several months ago with a seminarian in the middle of earning her
degree, we were talking about her recent experience of having
someone break into her e-mail. Of course, whenever someone
breaks into our safe places, we feel at the least insecure, and at the
worst violated and destroyed. What was interesting here, however,
was that she was furious that the president of the seminary had
preached a sermon on forgiveness, and had said that Christians
need to forgive those who sin against them. "He is so ridiculous,"
she said. "It's as though he thinks the burden of forgiveness is on
the shoulders of the person who has been wronged!" She got the
point and didn't like it one bit.

We cannot forgive unless we have been wronged. But what this
student was fully aware of was the shocking reality of the act of forgiving, when you no longer trust, when to forgive is to give up
things being made the way they were before we were wronged.
Forgiveness is an impossible human action because being wronged
means we are aware of what is right. Our refusal to "give in" is a
signal that we are fighting for justice on behalf of someone else or
for ourselves. Our resistance to forgiveness is our thought that if we
forgive, we are saying that this sinful, evil thing that worked
destruction is OK. We put forth demands that the other person show

repentance and make amends before asking for our forgiveness and before we forgive her. Forgiveness became a popular topic recently during the scandal of a president who was unfaithful to his wife and lied under oath. Many Christian ethicists said they could not and should not forgive him, because he was not truly repentant. But nowhere is this seen to be a requirement for forgiveness. In fact, Christ forgives without being asked to do so.

And Jesus Christ is the only reason we can live in the hope that forgiveness has to offer. Christ forgave without being asked to do so, but not without incredible cost—his very life. The offer of grace in Christ's work of reconciliation to God is the only thing that makes forgiveness possible. Forgiveness without this grace is impossible. It should be no surprise that forgiveness is an impossible human action, because it means taking this wrong thing into our own life and moving forward. This is only possible because Christ took all sin and evil into the divine life and overcame it. Following Christ means following in this way of reconciliation. This doesn't mean condoning sin or evil or suffering. These forces destroy the very human life God loves with endless passion. Nor does this mean forgetting wrong, if forgetting means ignoring it. Forgiveness requires that we tell the truth about sin.

The Christian understanding of forgiveness is based in the forgiveness of Christ who died and rose once for all. It is accomplished. But like all realities of Christian existence, the manifestation of the reality of forgiveness is a sure thing, but not yet complete. Jesus told us not that we should forgive once or seven times, but seventy times seven times—over and over again until we can't count. Forgiveness is not accomplished in one act. It takes repeated forgiveness. This is how parents and children can grow together. We don't stop our faults when we're forgiven, and the sins others commit against us continue even though they are truly repentant. We must forgive one another, over and over again. It takes time.

Like Christ we have to learn to forgive without being asked to do so. What we have received from Christ is forgiveness that was offered before we even knew we were sinners and lived in sin.

Grace is so very costly. Bonhoeffer says it well when he reminds us that when God bids us come and follow, God bids us to come and die. We die "to self," giving up the power over the control of existence. Grace costs us dearly when we learn to forgive. Forgiveness "does not insist on its own way; it is not irritable or resentful; it does not rejoice at wrong, but rejoices in the right. [It] bears all things, believes all things, hopes all things, endures all things" (1 Cor. 13:5–7).

Not that forgiving or following Christ in any other way is tantamount to self-destruction. Quite the opposite. In fact, we are told that the person who gives up her life for the sake of Christ finds it. But to follow Christ is to pick up our cross, to willingly follow a path that gives up control over how the world works, over how the justice of the universe plays out. The Holy Spirit brings us union with Christ, and in the sacrament of baptism we receive the sign of water which signifies the death, life, and resurrection we now share with Christ. What we die to is an old way of life, and our true life is found with Christ.

But this is in no way a call to suffer for the sake of suffering. Should someone who really wants to be forgiving deliberately put themselves in the way of those who would harm them? It is heresy to say that an abused wife (for example) should stay with her partner because she has a chance to forgive. Certainly, she has a chance to forgive, but that does not mean that she must forfeit her life. She could forgive just as readily in a safe place. We are not to seek our own destruction any more than we are to seek the destruction of others. God calls us to abundant life, not to a life that glorifies needless suffering. It is precisely because we seek the fullness of life with God, others, and the entire creation that we are called to forgiveness. What we die to is a life without God. What we live for is a life with God, the Divine who is the source of our being, and the source of all that is. We live mindful of all the human beings that God has created for joy and glory, and that we are part of this great reality.

But we live in the midst of cultures and people—ourselves!— who have to learn through sin and heartbreak what it is to live for good through God. Forgiveness is the power of reconciliation, made possible by Jesus Christ. Having received the grace of joy and the pleasure of generosity, we move forward with the necessary possibility of forgiveness so that we can maintain and heal the bonds that exist between human beings.

Forgiving is not the only thing we need to learn how to do. As people who are at the same time sinless and sinners, we must learn day by day how to live as human beings created and called by God.

4

God Reaches Out to Us

What God Does

I am a Christian because I need God.

I am a Christian because in the grace of the Lord Jesus Christ, the love of God, and the communion of the Holy Spirit I discover the overflowing life of the one who loves and forgives us in truth.

I am a Christian because through the sacraments God reaches out to me and makes the mysterious grace of the Divine something I can touch and something I can share with others.

A few Sundays ago, in church, we celebrated both baptism and the Lord's Supper, and, as my nephew once said, "My heart was so full it came out my eyes." Witnessing the baptism of a little child, seeing the tangible declaration of God's astonishing and intimate love for that precious person, is always an affirmation to me that God has first loved me. Then, upon that promise, to partake of the bread and the wine, to chew upon the sustaining life of the one who is for me and with me and who binds me with all that is God's, I was struck. My heart was strangely and marvelously warmed. I am a Christian because I need the sacraments.

These reminders—the water and the bread and the wine—are objective and tangible evidence to me. They are tokens in our life which can take us to what is fundamentally true and good about being human. Out of the mundane, unnoticed presence of my wedding band I am suddenly seeing it shine, and I'll take it off and read with pleasure and assurance the engraving with which my husband surprised me. And back it goes on my finger, this gift he gave and gives. Or I see the collage of black-and-white photos my father took of the four of us kids when we were young, and I can see his love of us through the lens of his camera, and I'm reminded of the blessing of my family. Right now, on top of my computer rests my first pair of those Groucho Marx nose-and-glasses, given to me by my horrified ("What do you mean, you don't have a nose-and-glasses?") youth minister friends during seminary days. In the midst of my vocational angst they gave me more of my humor, and they rooted me to the ground.

All these tokens remind me of who these people are *for* me, what they have given to me, how they have structured and formed my life. There are times when we doubt God's goodness, doubt God's love, think God's promises might not be for us. There are times when we know—without a doubt—God's goodness, love, and promises, and we smile as we rejoice. The sacraments are means of grace. They confirm to us, no matter how we feel at the time, that there's nothing we can do to make God love us more, and there's nothing we can do to make God love us less, as Philip Yancey has so eloquently put it. The sacraments are the very grace of God, the promise of God, the covenant of God made flesh in Jesus Christ to free us from sin and death and free us for abundant and joyful life. The sacraments are the very grace of God that we can touch and taste and feel. God's promises to us come from outside ourselves: They expand our life into the divine life, reconciling us to God, ourselves, each other, and the entire creation. Truly, God has done marvelous things.

And that is why I rejoice in the sacraments.

God's Good Work

Christ died for us when we were yet sinners. Christ did this knowing what he was to do, and he was willing to do it. In the Lord's Supper and baptism we sit at the table with Christ and his disciples and we stand beside the river. Jesus was baptized and he shared meals. The sacraments bring us into union with God through Jesus Christ by the power of the Holy Spirit in an earthy and vivid way, just as they remind us of Christ's humanness; for Jesus experienced—and was the power behind—these sacramental actions, too.

Jesus felt the water on his body, Jesus chewed the bread and tasted the wine. In different ways, these two sacraments—baptism and the Lord's Supper—were ways that God, in, with, and through Jesus Christ, communicated the divine presence, which is the divine promise to be with us, lo, even unto the end of the age. In different ways, the sacraments continually present to us the hope of those who follow Christ. While we are baptized only once we renew and reaffirm our baptism every time a new person receives baptism. We partake of the Lord's Supper often, and we do both of these things until God comes again. All along, we are reminded that the work is God's work and that all we have to do is receive the promise and the blessing and the hope of reconciliation with God through Christ.

It Was God's Work
in the Beginning, Anyway

So why should we be fainthearted? Our union with God and with one another is something God accomplishes. Because we are created, we are dependent upon God for our existence. Surely, our earthly and earthy life is good—in Jesus Christ this was overwhelmingly affirmed. But this is exactly why we have to remember that we can never make ourselves or our life good on our own. We are good, life is good, because we are with God; we are good, not because we are perfect or the best, but because God says, "It is good."

John Calvin calls the sacraments "helps" because they strengthen us in a vivid way. We need them because we need God and because, without them, our faith is weak. The sacraments give us life, warm our souls, touch and become one with our bodies, and by the power of the Holy Spirit seal the promise of God's union with us through Jesus Christ.

My husband has a very hard time surprising me. I am just good at figuring things out, watching for signs, solving puzzles. So a few years ago when he made sure I got out of the house, I just *knew* he was trying to do a good job of wrapping my present.

I was very pleased of course, but also a bit frustrated. "Why on earth," I wondered, "couldn't he just close a door to one of the rooms?" We were living in an attic artist's-garret apartment at the time, with small rooms at odd angles, up and down an odd little pair of stairs, so he should have been able to wrap covertly. But I sighed with the sure, patient knowledge of a young wife that my husband just needed as much space and privacy as possible since he was new at wrapping things for his beloved.

I remember shaking my head knowingly, and yes, smugly, as I walked to the library to study for a couple of hours. Studying was hard, of course, but I waited (I was being so indulgent) and then walked home through the not-yet-cold December air, up the several, angled, steep staircases in the old home, opened the door to our landing, went up another staircase, then another landing, then up the last three steps, around the corner, to the left toward the dark living room (Where was Doug?), and

"SURPRISE!!!"

The room was full of family and friends, there to celebrate my thirtieth birthday. I was stunned, (nearly) speechless, and positively delighted. What a marvelous surprise, a perfect gift. What a fun evening. Even my brother had come in from New York City to join the festivities. In our tiny, cramped apartment friends gathered and ate and drank and laughed and talked and shared. What bliss.

"SURPRISE!!!"

God is waiting around the corner. And God is already with you at home. God is at the table and at the fountain to bless you, reassure you, gather you with the community of faith, and actually *touch* you with water, bread, and wine. God makes that happen for you and for me in so many ways, and so tangibly in the sacraments. God does this for us. The grace of the Lord Jesus Christ, the love of God, and the communion of the Holy Spirit is with us all.

And that's why I'm a Christian.

What We Do

My niece Elizabeth just turned five, and although I hate to say good-bye to her littleness, both in size and girlhood, it is delightful to begin entering into conversations with her and get to know her as a person. It was when she was three and a half that it became clear that she had a great gift for delightful gab and for stories. No doubt this is due to her memory, a memory that can hold on to and relate stories in minute detail, stories from nearly two years ago. Her stories are always triggered by something flying in out of left field and begin, "Y'member, Mom? 'member, Dad? 'member when we went to the hotel and I wanted to go swimming but the pool was closed and I was very sad but the lady at the counter was nice and she gave me . . ." and on and on and on. Sometimes she reminds my brother and sister-in-law of things they would rather forget, as many kids do. "Y'member when you went away and left me alone with Grammy and Grampy and I was very sad? 'member?"

Elizabeth can sit in your lap, happy as a clam (which she likes to eat very much), trusting you completely, smiling and giggling (which she also likes very much), and tell you all about the time she was left alone and the other time she was sad, and the different times she was scared. *She remembers*, because they are part of her history and part of her life. Somehow Elizabeth has the gift of remembering all the stories. When she went to the hotel (you remember the one, the pool was closed and she was very sad but the lady at the counter was nice and she gave her . . .), she was going to a party for her aunt whom she took to calling "Dokor Selly," and what a fun party it was. *She remembers*, and nothing is left out, and she uses all these memories as a rich part of her present and future experiences. When she remembers her life through the telling of her stories, she knits together all the different parts of her experience, and because she does this out of generosity—wanting to share every bit with you, the story hearer—she creates an expectancy for a future of more rich memories.

What better exemplar could we have for the sacraments than Elizabeth? We are called to do them in remembrance of Christ and what he did for us. These signs of the creation God brought into being are helps to us, concrete connections to the work of God that help us remember and tell the story of our own life, which is grounded in the life-giving work of God in Jesus Christ. Remembering Christ's work in the sacraments helps us to understand our own life, to form the way we live. We come to these sacraments remembering the good and the bad, the sins we have committed, the sins that have been committed against us, our broken hearts, our joys and loves and delights. Christ knits all these together into something more grand than we could have made on our own: Christ is the one who declares what the shape of our lives is, who draws us into a story of richness and joy and fellowship.

We are blessed by the divine Creator of all that is, and we are reassured through these sacraments. We are created, saved, and sanctified by the triune God. We are not left on our own in sin and despair and difficulties, afflicted by our own failings or the failings of others. We are not alone. Such is the magnificence of the triune God, who is *not alone*. To be created in the image of God means that we are in the company of God and others, for to be human means by definition that we are connected to God and to other human beings. This fellowship was not added as an afterthought.

As Christians we believe that God has always been triune, for instance, that "in the beginning was the Word, and the Word was with God, and the Word was God" (John 1:1). Jesus Christ was not invented to take care of us, like Q-tips were invented to clean out ears. Christ existed from the beginning. We see God's purpose for humankind throughout the Old Testament and the New Testament, in the earnest and passionate actions of a God whose desire is for God's people to live together in peace and justice so that they (and now we) can glorify God together forever.

Thus, in the hymn "Amazing Grace" after we celebrate the fact that we were lost and now are found, we finally sing,

> When we've been there ten thousand years,
> Bright shining as the sun,
> We've no less days to sing God's praise
> Than when we'd first begun.

The salvation that God promises and gives voluntarily is salvation for a people God loves and desires, for human beings God has created.

Grace: The Salvation of Jesus Christ, the One Who Called God "Abba"

My husband and I, while trying to make a connecting flight through the Minneapolis airport, were faced with yet another long trek. This was an annoying and frequent occurrence during which we could almost always guarantee that we would have to walk from gate 1 to gate 75 within a half hour.

Fortunately, Minneapolis has those human conveyor belts. This is fortunate because, for my husband, they're a great big toy and his mood is lightened instantly. It is also fortunate because it halves your walking time.

On this particular occasion, however, we got stuck behind a father and his daughter. They weren't really particularly slow, but they were hard to pass because the daughter was frolicking about, looking here and there. In one of those notes you make to yourself, we silently observed that they were Jewish, since he was wearing a yarmulke. Doug and I were both trying to maintain our patience at their leisurely pace (a spiritual gift neither one of us holds in abundance), when the happy daughter, looking out the window at an enormous airplane taking off, said "Abba, Abba, look!" "Yes, sweetheart," he responded, "it's a big plane." And she took his hand and walked merrily along. Doug and I looked at each other in wonderment, suddenly calling to our minds that verse in Romans 8 where we read that we are God's own children and call God Abba, and we both thought, "So that's what it means."

The intimacy of Jesus with God is of this nature, of the loving parent with his beloved child, an intimacy of joy, boldness, candor, delight, trust. This is what Jesus called God. Abba—the name that your everyday, happy, frolicking Jewish girl uses for the father with whom she shares her joy as they walk through an airport. It is magnificent, and it is mundane. It is awesome and average. Through this intimacy—which we ourselves know through both presence and absence of parental love—God portrayed God's love for human beings. This bond of God with Christ is the bond of God with all of us, for we Christians believe that Christ was the new Adam, the new humankind, in whom all humans are caught up.

Of course the intimacy between God and Jesus Christ is also entirely different from the intimacy between a parent and a child, since it is the intimacy of the Godhead. God the Father and Jesus Christ the Son are God together with the Holy Spirit, the Spirit who binds us to God, reconciling us in Christ to God. The bond of love is fabulous and fierce, for it is pure grace. Giving us life, God restores our life through Christ, drawing us to the Divine as a mother nurses her child.

It is in the life, death, and resurrection of Jesus Christ that we see most clearly—or at least most easily—who God is and who God is toward us. Of course, this is not without the power of the Holy Spirit who works within each one of us to bring us to faith that we cannot come to on our own. It is the Holy Spirit who helps us to see Jesus Christ as fully God and fully human, and therefore to see the miracle of salvation by grace through faith alone, the salvation that we cannot work for ourselves.

Through the grace of Jesus Christ, we are restored to fellowship with God, and through the Holy Spirit we are upheld in this fellowship, nurtured, taught, and comforted as sinners who are redeemed and in the presence of the triune God. We are not alone. Our sin has not cut us off, finally, from the love of God (Rom. 8).

This, then, is the first and most important help we have in our Christian understanding of our response to God's creation and our call into God's work for the world. We are not alone, we are not self-sufficient, we are not taking a test. Instead, as we seek to live our lives, day by day, we are in fellowship and we are upheld, whether we feel it or not.

Our God is good, and has given us what the church has traditionally called "helps" for living our lives as Christians. These things—the church and the sacraments—are blessed to us and powered for us by the Holy Spirit.

The Help of the Sacraments

I referred earlier to the apostle Paul's reminder that we have one faith, one Lord, one baptism. The baptism of which he speaks is the baptism of the Holy Spirit, symbolized in the Christian church by water. What does this sacrament—and the other Protestant sacrament of the Lord's Supper—mean for the Christian understanding of being a person?* How is it a help to being a person?

Let's begin with the Lord's Supper, or the celebration of the Eucharist. "Eucharist" means "thanksgiving." The Great Prayer of Thanksgiving is included in many liturgies for the celebration of the Lord's Supper. It begins,

> The Lord be with you.
> *And also with you.*
> Lift up your hearts.
> *We lift them to the Lord.*

In these phrases we thank God for giving us the great sacrifice of Christ's body and blood. We thank God for this gift and for the miracle of the resurrection. When we participate in the Lord's Supper, we remember Christ until he comes again. We remember that Jesus Christ's body has been broken and Christ's blood has been poured out for us.

The sacrament of the Lord's Supper is not a celebration of death and destruction, however. The destruction of Christ's body and the shedding of his blood are not important in and of themselves, but because God in Jesus Christ offered the divine self up to death in order to defeat death on our behalf, to intervene so that our death would not mean our separation from God. We have to be careful not to celebrate with great joy the destruction of any human body, and the church has tended to hold up suffering as honorable in and of itself. The reason we want to avoid this is that Christ is

---

*Within the Christian church there are two main traditions. These are the Catholic and the Protestant traditions. Protestants affirm two sacraments: baptism and the Lord's Supper, or Eucharist. Catholics affirm seven sacraments: baptism, confirmation, the Eucharist, reconciliation, anointing of the sick, marriage, and ordination.

not *for* suffering: Christ's work is to reconcile human beings to God and ultimately Christians hope for a world where no one is hungry, where no one sins, where God is the ruler over all and God's work of justice has been accomplished. What is important about Christ's broken body and shed blood is that Jesus, fully God and fully human, *chose* to submit his body and soul—his entire self—to this condition of sin and death in order that death would not be the final word in our lives. This is why death has lost its sting.

If we allow ourselves to think that suffering in and of itself is good, we can let ourselves off the hook while we stand by and watch others suffer, or we will allow ourselves to suffer when the action that would glorify God would be to remove ourselves from this suffering. Nor is suffering something we can require of others so that they are more godlike. We must confront ourselves with our own arrogance if we sit in our comfortable lives while someone else is suffering, comforting ourselves and them (supposedly) with the thought that their suffering purifies them or brings them closer to God.

Contrary to this destructive form of suffering is the suffering exemplified by Christ, who "knowing that equality with God was not a thing to be grasped, emptied himself." Here Christ does not sacrifice others; he puts himself forward to a particular kind of task and does what is required of that task. People do not become teachers in order that they may have the chance to suffer. However, teachers may find themselves in a situation in which they are threatened by a student, at odds with the school board, or cut out of a job because of decreasing funds. Suffering is inevitable for Christians who take up their cross and follow Christ, not because suffering in and of itself is good, but because following Christ in the midst of a sinful world means things are going to happen that hurt us. When we remember Christ's sacrifice in the Lord's Supper, we remember the gift and the choice of God to be for us, to give his life for us that we might be reconciled to God.

A second thing we have to remember is that Christ's body is broken and his blood is shed for us. Not for me, for us. *Us* includes me, but is not limited to me. The salvation of God in Jesus Christ is personal but it is not private. It is for me, but not for me alone. This is why the Lord's Supper, or the Eucharist, is also called "Communion." We are engrafted into the community of the body of Christ when we participate in the Lord's Supper.

As a person, I come to the Lord's Supper to be fed, to be brought into the body of Christ. I myself am broken. Christ came for me, a sinner, to make me one of God's own, to bring me into the fold, to nourish me and sustain me, and to remind me of Christ's amazing generosity.

I have heard so many good sermons in my time, sermons which in a twinkling changed my understanding of something or turned on a light in my brain. But there are only about two sermons that I remember specifically. One of these was a Communion sermon, preached by one of my fellow students at seminary. She was preaching about the feast of the Lord, and her example for this particular sermon was the movie *Babette's Feast*. In this movie, a woman who has escaped war in France becomes the servant of two spinsters in Denmark. For various reasons, she cooks a gourmet meal that almost brings one person at the dinner to tears of joy. The individuals at this table, eating this food, have vowed not to enjoy it because it is decadent and indulgent, rather than moderate and sober and practical.

These cranky people come to the table bound and determined not to enjoy themselves or to enjoy the food. But a miracle happens. One of their number has been to France, and he knows the magnificent food they enjoy there. He enjoyed it himself. He is amazed at the exquisite blending of flavors, perfectly matched with wine. He is overcome by the presence of such beauty in a place where he had not seen beauty and in a place where he had been surrounded by self-denial and self-doubt. The food moves him to proclaim the blessedness of life, the truth that justice and peace will embrace, that goodness will overcome all. Slowly, throughout the meal, all the people begin to melt into one another through forgiveness and reconciliation and humor. And this all comes about through a meal that has taken every last penny and demanded immense labor of the chef, resources and effort that are required when one puts on a meal of this nature.

It was a wonderful image of Communion, made even more wonderful by actually taking Communion that day. And when the grape juice hit the back of my throat I was reminded of what a feast does: it makes you want more, even while it comforts and fills you.

So Communion is something we participate in again and again, to see God's nourishment, to be reminded of who we are, to solidify the ties with which Christ has bound us in freedom to God's own self and to one another. Here, in this sacrament, we are reminded of how precious each one of us is to God, and how in being reconciled we are saved not apart from others, but into, with, and for others, an entire community of precious individuals. Like my niece, we remember not just what God has done, but what God is doing and will do. By participating, we anticipate the Christian hope of the Messianic banquet, when God reconciles us and all creation by the power of the Spirit through Christ.

Baptism

Just this Sunday we were visiting friends in Bismarck, and Jim, who is a pastor there, baptized a baby. He did something I have never seen a pastor do: He kissed the baby on the forehead.

Baptisms pull tears out of me every time anyway, but this took the cake. He greeted this child with a holy kiss, declaring the tenderness that exists on the part of God who is our "Abba," our parent who loves us with steadfastness, strength, and tenderness. Welcoming a child or an adult into the church with baptism is not merely a sign that "your membership application has been approved." It is entering into a whole new life. The sacrament of baptism isn't a trite reason for a family gathering but a sign that we as a congregation will bring this child up, and nurture this person into a life of discipleship. On behalf of this person, we promise to recognize the earthly sign of water as conveying the action of God to wipe away the sins of the world and the sins of this one person, and the action of God to bind this person to God's very own self in a covenant of grace. We recognize through this earthly sign that this person is not on her own, but is a child of God.

As Christians, baptism reminds us of what it means to be a person. Baptism reminds us that we are created, called, redeemed, and sanctified. The history of the Christian faith becomes our history, the history of Noah and the flood, of John's baptism of Jesus. Our liturgy at baptism reminds us of the history of our own life, that we have been created by God, that we are God's very own, and that we are brought into the covenant God made with Abraham and Sarah. In baptism we receive the promise of Christ. God has promised that this action is a means of grace, that the water really does make tangible and real the promise of Christ for our life and death.

One of my favorite seminary professors always complained that Presbyterians didn't use nearly enough water. He didn't mean just a generous sprinkling instead of a wet-nap one. He meant LOTS of water. He thought we should be pouring gallons and gallons over those people—children and adults—who were getting baptized. Why be so stingy with the grace we are promised?

This water doesn't just symbolize a nice little ritual of acceptable membership in our little church community. This water symbolizes death. In baptism we die with Christ. We die to sin and death. This is why either the person being baptized or her guardian has to answer some form of the question "Do you renounce all evil, and powers in the world which defy God's righteousness and love?" Water can kill.

And without water there is no human life. This water doesn't just symbolize that someone now is a member in good standing. This water symbolizes life that overcomes death, the life of God in Christ without which there is no human life. This is why my professor was so adamant about LOTS of water. It's in the abundance of the water that we can understand so vividly what the meaning of that earthly element is.

Those of us writing books for this series were commissioned in a service of worship. We were exhorted to live out our baptism in this task, our call to be disciples of Christ, and to proclaim the good news of the gospel for all people. The liturgist led us through the prayer of confession, and out of the time of silence that followed, with our heads bowed and eyes closed as we waited for the assurance of pardon, we suddenly heard water falling, echoing vividly and languidly throughout the chapel. "Hear the good news of the gospel." Like a brook that babbles without haste through a flowered meadow on a soft summer's day, that water falling off her fingers as she dipped them into the font brought the feel of cool water to our toes and throats. This water satisfies thirst, and brings pardon and cleansing and delight.

The Body of Christ:
The Church and the Christian Person

When we are baptized, we are called to the priesthood of all believers. Our baptism does not signify the grace that we receive as individuals, but rather that we are received as individuals into the community of faith grounded in Jesus Christ. The church is the body of Christ for us, making possible our life with the triune God. But the church is not something just invented to make us feel better. The church grows out of who God is and who Christ is, and we are bound together in the church through who the Holy Spirit is.

When we first looked at being created *imago Dei*, we noted at once that this means to be created as human beings, not as one single person. Human beings were created as two individuals who *together* make up what it means to be human (see Gen. 1:27). The body of Christ gives us a chance to live this way. It is not only because we need the strength and support of one another to live human life, but because of the vast richness of the body of Christ. The fact that we are all individuals and each one of us is unique is not a hindrance to God's work. This infinite variety is, in fact, the precise way in which God's work is done. It is the possibility of fulfillment of the body of Christ, not its destruction. In the church we can draw on the resources of one another. Even more, the church also exists as the space for humans to be fully human!

Because the church is full of unique persons, it is full of great diversity and difference. This diversity is demonstrated by opinions about everything from what kind of coffee is appropriate for church fellowship (caffeine or "why bother"), to what makes a member, what to teach children, and even who should be ordained. The diversity of the church includes different denominations, different theological viewpoints, different races, different backgrounds, different economic situations, different political views, different styles of worship. With all these differences, what unites the church? What makes the church *the* church is not us, but God.

This is why Paul writes in Ephesians that "there is one body and one Spirit, just as you were called to the one hope of your calling, one Lord, one faith, one baptism, one God and Father of all, who is above all and through all and in all" (Eph. 4:4–6). It is not our conformity to ideas or theology, or our conformity to one another, which unites us. It is God, the triune God alone, who forms the church as Christ's body through the power of the Holy Spirit.

But what good is the church? Fair question! For many of us do not feel helped at all in our churches. Instead we feel frustrated, either because no one is interested in us and what's happening in our lives, or because we can't get the work done that the church wants us to get done because people keep getting in our way. There are a couple of things we have to remember here.

First, the church of Jesus Christ is not limited to one local congregation. All our faith should not be based on the particular congregation of which we are members. No one congregation is exclusively the true church, and any church that thinks it is is suffering delusions of grandeur (we say this remembering we all suffer delusions of something). It may be that our own congregation knows too much or too little about us, and that in the midst of some struggle we are working through, someone from another church or beyond the church is God's minister to us. The power of the church to be a fellowship is from God alone, we must remember.

Second, the persons whom God has created and called may not be members of our local churches. This does not mean that God is not working through them. The point of being Christian within the church is not so that we can neatly define, for ourselves and others, what it means to be Christian. Rather, the point of being Christian within the church is to understand ourselves as a fellowshiping

body of people who recognize that the force at work in the world
to make human life human is not some vague idea of God, but the
God we know is Father, Son, and Holy Spirit, the God with a name
who walks among us, the particular God who shelters us warmly
like a mother hen.

This *koinonia* is the community of believers who witness to the
saving action of God in Christ, the community of believers building one another up for the joy of glorifying the Creator and the delight of being witness for the sake of others. The *koinonia* is the
community of individuals who together live in the world for the sake
of the world, enjoying the world as God's gift, and who work to
serve the world. The *koinonia* is the community of believers who
now see with simplicity, never able to see the world without God
nor God without the world, since in Christ God has reconciled all
things to God's own self.

But the *koinonia* is not separate from the world, not against it.
Christians who identify themselves as members of the believing
community also understand themselves as bound up with all other
human beings, so that every single human being is our neighbor.
So what is fundamentally human in human beings is vast and rich
and diverse—vast even to eternity. It is the gift from God to human
beings of a power for life and fullness, a power that allows
human beings to be and to fulfill themselves in and through relationships of dependence and self-giving toward God and others.
This is not the dependence in which we give up the self: This is the
dependence that recognizes that we have a self, and that this self is
connected to others. That's why maturity, for Christians, is *self-
acceptance through self-giving*.

Who is the person who shows more integrity: the one who never
swears and heartily disapproves of others who do? or the person
who swears occasionally and never puts another person down? We
do not reach Christian maturity by ourselves. There is no pillar of
the church community who became such a supporting strength on
her own. Those people we look to as exemplars of faith did not
carve themselves out of marble and erect themselves to support the
structure of the church. It was others who taught them in Sunday

school, loved them, encouraged them, strengthened them in hard times. Pillars are erected by construction workers, who were taught by others, and supported by still others, not the least of which is the Holy Spirit!

Christians mature as a body matures, each individual part growing together, having growth spurts at different times but all working together. In a human body, if one part matures and nothing else does, the body is sick and needs help. This is "the good of all in the good of each."

This understanding of human maturity, self-acceptance through self-giving, is a response to Christ's own generosity. Drawing on the significance of the individuals who comprise the community, we must emphasize the vastness of Christ's gift. The uniqueness of individuality is as infinite as the human race, and Christians affirm that this diversity, instead of making Christian life chaotic, actually makes it orderly, since each human being in the body of Christ is a necessary part of the body of Christ. Without this vast array of individuality, the church would not be fulfilled.

An excellent example of Christian maturity can be seen in teenagers and youth groups. Teenagers are passionate about self-acceptance through self-giving. Of course, this is one of the reasons teenagers find themselves cautioned so much, for the same instinct of self-acceptance through self-giving that fuels commitments to the underprivileged is also the instinct that drives toward careless and self-destructive sex. Take a look at the teenagers and college students around you. You see them on work trips, volunteering, you see them frustrated by wrongs in the world. When encouraged, we see the dramatic feats that youth are capable of, their unflagging energy.

This is seen even more clearly when compared to the dark side of young life, when self-rejection through destruction manifests itself in the shootings in our inner cities and in high schools, when sex leads to death and abandonment and illness, when self-acceptance is sublimated into acceptance by others and judged by drinking and raping, when there is no self without the approval of others.

But youth are not one thing, and we must not give in to the

temptation to label each and every person under the age of twenty-six as Generation X (or Y or Me or what have you). Youth are not one thing. The variety of youth is as astoundingly complex and rich as the variety of thirty-year-olds or five-year-olds or seventy-eight-year-olds. And if we observe the youth in our churches carefully, we will see that many of our youth are well on their way to maturity while many of us are far behind.

If a human person is being created in the image of God, free for God and for others, and if maturity is self-giving through self-acceptance, then we have to take seriously how we understand the church. How does this understanding help us to focus our ministry with, to, and for one another?

It makes us realize that the life of the church is concrete. It is real people, real individuals, not some mysterious institution out there like we often think of our government. And if the life of the church is concrete and particular, not some formal way of doing things, then our lives with one another take on all sorts of rich color. Our children clap their hands together with interlocking fingers and say, "Here's the church," with their hands together, "and here's the steeple," with their index fingers pointing skyward. Then they move their thumbs, "Open the doors," and wiggle the rest of their fingers, "and see all the people!"

Safe in the hand of the little child are the people. Christians claim in song that God "has the whole world in his hands." Ministry in the church for the sake of the world is a ministry in which Christians live out the safety of human life, by making human life safe, by prospering the life of all people. People at all stages of life teach of the importance of this ministry of safety in the face of the vulnerability of three-year-olds and eighty-year-olds and sixteen-year-olds, of the vulnerability of those who are poor in our congregation, and of those who give way too much of themselves on the path to their own demise, of families stressed to the point of breaking, couples stressed to parting, people stressed to dying. Within the church and without, wickedness and weakness creep in. The gift of Christ is to enable us to fulfill ourselves by being the individuals that we are for the sake of others.

God is not limited to the church, nor is God limited by the church. We are not the last bastion of God's people on earth. The church need not be threatened by rifts or disagreements or petty differences, because the church is not founded on human beings. It is founded on Christ. Do we think Christ is threatened by non-Christians, by ideas that seem to us to be evil or heretical? Certainly not—*this is precisely whom Christ is for*. We never know whom God is going to use for God's work or on our behalf.

Third, while the church is full of imperfect people, we can rejoice that we are simultaneously redeemed and sinners. Not even that horrible, cranky, nasty person who always sits in that pew over there is separated from the love of God (no matter how much we are separated from him or her). And so we are amazed that the old woman who always looks down her nose at certain people, who insists stubbornly that people who sin are going to hell, is the one person who put her arm around the single mother who walked into the congregation ashamed. And we are amazed that the fourteen-year-old boy who is always getting into trouble, swearing in Sunday school, getting picked up by police, and is a discipline problem in school, makes an immediate connection with the old man leaving church and falling down the stairs with his walker. And we are amazed when we find out that ditzy Mrs. Smith, who walks around "without the sense that God gave a goose," is the cheery, light person who was a beacon to her neighbor, finally beckoning her to church. And we are amazed that the arrogant young man who is the associate minister turns out to be the one who talks sense into hardhearted Mr. Jones.

All of us have stories of this nature. And the list goes on and on and on of the frail, faulty, and finite human beings whose work dovetails with the work of others to create something magnificent. God often surprises us with our churches and in our churches. We need to remember that we are chosen—we don't do the choosing—and we are chosen for our sake and for the sake of others.

This means, finally, that while the church is for us, it is not only a resource there to meet our individual needs, like me reaching for my bottle of Ibuprofen when I have a headache. The church—the body of Christ—is for us and we are for it. Those other people in our local congregation are not just for us, we are for them. As individual members of the body of Christ, we are for those other members who may not look so good to us. In an age where we are confronted with so much exhortation to self-fulfillment and self-actualization, it is difficult for us to remember that Christian maturity is self-acceptance through self-giving; it is the good of all in the good of each. We are called to this for each one of us, ourselves and others. The church is a help to us because God works through each one of us for each one of us.

5

Goodness outside the Garden

What can there be worthwhile in life outside the garden? After Adam and Eve separate themselves from God, is there any hope for a life of richness, or abundance or grace or goodness? Is there any hope for goodness in life for those of us who have sinned and fallen short?

Ah, the goodness of God. Remember, Adam and Eve put themselves on a level with their Creator by claiming they could decide what God meant by the divine command *not* to eat of the tree of the knowledge of good and evil. And by doing this, they severed themselves from their life source, from that necessary Creator-creature relationship, by thinking they could be their own gods, their own creators. In Genesis 3:22 we see God's mercy, albeit ironically displayed. God does not want Adam and Eve to live forever apart from the divine presence, apart from the ground of their life. This is the God who called humans into existence as the very reflection of God's image. And so God, afraid Adam and Eve will also eat of the tree of life and live forever in this separated state, cuts them out of the Garden of Eden and guards it with fire.

God does not destroy Adam and Eve. God clothes them, so they no longer face God's presence with shame. God gives them earth, God gives them pain, and God gives them each other, despite the fact that they now live unto themselves in sin instead of for God and for each other.

No doubt we live in this pain, just as Adam and Eve did, and God gives us each other, despite our inherent tendencies to put ourselves above others, and God gives us the earth in which to live, despite the fact that we must wrestle with it while depending on it. Through all of this we know the goodness of God in Jesus Christ, who is our clothing against shame. Goodness is possible outside the garden because we follow Jesus Christ who is leading us back to our origin, to God, to reconciled union with the Divine, with ourselves, with each other, with the entire creation. The Peaceable Kingdom is the gift of Christ. Goodness is possible because God is with us.

Providence

Part of goodness outside the garden is what Dietrich Bonhoeffer called "the orders of preservation." Some people say that the curse for Adam and Eve is the design God set down for human interaction. But Bonhoeffer points out that humans are to interact depending on how God is working and what God is commanding at any given time. God doesn't give a command or set some law down and then exit stage left to see what this comedy troupe of human beings does. Instead God constantly acts within human history and the life of creation to bring it to the fulfillment of God's intention for it. God's attention to us is not distracted, wavering, uncaring, or cruel. Rather, God preserves the creation out of love for it, continuing to love it, no matter how much agony God's people cause.

God will not let us go because each one of us has been created for God's work. The Creator who created us, called us, and loves us is the one who sustains us and strengthens us. We Christians believe that God is at work in the world for the good of the world, and the good of the world is caught up in God's plan for all creation. This is what we call providence. God is working out a plan and is bringing the kingdom of heaven to fruition. And the individual calling of each of us is bound up in the accomplishment of this work.

Sometimes the doctrine of providence becomes quite troublesome for us. When someone is suffering from a terrible tragedy it is easy to respond with "God will work it all out in the end." Or we say, "This will all turn out for good. You'll see." The problem is that we can use it to ignore our responsibilities to God and to others. It is true that "we know that all things work together for good for those who love God" (Rom. 8:28) but this does not let us off of any hook. Bonhoeffer said that the word of God is never about something or someone else, but about and *to me*. John Calvin is known for his extensive work on providence, but he never intended it to be used to ignore our love for our neighbor. When we can see that the mother of twins three doors down is suffering from manic depression, we offer to sit her kids, make meals, help in whatever needs to happen for healing to take place in that family. We don't simply say to her husband, "God's at work in this. You'll see." What he has just seen is a person calling herself a Christian who walked away from his need. Providence, for Calvin, was what we needed to remind ourselves of when life was hard. But this was a reminder for ourselves, and our connection to God, each other, and all creation.

We are part of God's providence for the world. This is not because we saunter on over to God's office, knock on the door, and say, "Hey, God, I have some free time this weekend and I've decided to help you with your providence work. I have some skills and abilities I think you will find quite useful." We are part of God's providence because *God* has made it so. This is what our callings are. Where would we be without God's providence through others?

This providence through others is not to be underestimated, and when we deliberately look for it, we see it in actions and events that seem mundane. My husband and I can testify to God's providence through normal, everyday events and actions. Just about our favorite thing during my doctoral work was evenings with the Demings. It was their house that held our cramped garret apartment, and as God's providence would have it, we got along well. Although we helped each other out, there is no doubt in our minds that we were the ones being provided for. Graduate work was no picnic, but we could always count on normalcy and peace in the household of that loving, chaotic family of two busy adults and two active children. Sharing red wine and snacks around the island in the kitchen, we could talk about our days, our stress, our dreams, the Seahawks and the Chargers, literature, and history; and in the middle of it all, we would laugh hard. Jacob would unselfconsciously climb into our laps and rub our necks while we read him a story, or Hannah's big gray-blue eyes would shimmer with the great thing she did in her soccer game. All this, plus Jamey's gourmet meals and Christie's hysterical anecdotes assured us that human existence—and our existence in particular—was OK.

Sometimes what God does for us through others takes the shape of big things—like a job, or a marriage—but much more often, providence comes in small, everyday, simple actions. Those times we shared with our friends—and the times we have shared with other friends and family—are times that most people experience. They're normal, expected, part of life. But God uses those times, uses us, and uses others to make those times experiences of God's love and goodness. But these don't happen by accident. I'm struck by this often as a teacher. I'll be going along, lecturing, filling in my planned material with a bit of extemporaneous wit, and think nothing of it. Then a few weeks or months later, a student writes a note or turns in a paper where one phrase or sentence I said turned him around and did something good for him. Good doesn't accidentally happen: The good I can do in the classroom comes from the fact that God works through it and I get out of the way.

Sometimes, though, I don't get out of the way. If I'm not careful, and if I don't train myself to be *for* my neighbor (my student, my spouse, my colleague, the cashier), the little things that I do can work against God's providence. What I do with my actions can make God look like a liar. The habits we practice, the things we do, and the small steps we take in ordinary, everyday life, as Aristotle observed, make all the difference.

And if calling is a day-by-day path made up of small steps following the call of God on the way ahead, then our participation in God's providence for the world is made up of smaller things as well. By answering God's call to make casseroles for families who have loved ones in the hospital, we are participating in God's providence. By being mechanics who do everything we can to make a car safe and sound, we are using our unique skills and gifts to participate in God's providence for the world.

The good news of the gospel, though, is that God's care and love do not depend on us. God may work through us, but God is not bound by us. God works divine care for creation in surprising ways. In a class I team-taught on economics and ethics, we required the students to serve twice at a homeless shelter in town that provided evening meals. Several of the students wrote in a subsequent paper about how surprised they were to learn that they had a lot in common with those who were homeless. The only real difference between them and the homeless was that they had homes and food and the others didn't. They realized they were all human beings. At the beginning, many of these students thought that the homeless deserved what they got. These students moved to a point where they cared deeply about other human beings simply because they were human. They all wrote that they fully intended to continue serving their communities in this way. How did God help these students open themselves up to compassion? How did they learn about their common humanity? Because these students, all of whom are pro-wrestling fans, discovered that the men in the shelter enjoyed watching professional wrestling on the shelter television, just like they did, and knew all the different wrestlers, just like these college students did. Through professional wrestling God is taking care of the world? Now *that's* a miracle.

In order to act in such a way that we love our neighbor for Christ's sake, that we participate in God's care for the world, we need to pay attention to God. We are not left with the skeleton of an instruction, "God is good and loves you." We know through Scripture and Jesus Christ and the testimony of the Holy Spirit just what this love looks like, and just how God cares and directs us to care for one another. The laws of God free us precisely through reminding us of our limits. Beyond these limits we become godless, misanthropic islands cut off from community. Our actions matter very much, and God has not left us without wisdom as to what comprises good, human, reconciled life.

What makes the vast array of human activity work for the sake of the world is not necessarily the honor of the work, or its prestige, but the fact that *God makes it work*. We do not bring all these different callings together—God does. And even though we affirm the worth of all human beings because it is declared by God, even though we know we are uniquely loved, created, and cherished, we know that we are a part and not the whole. We Christians believe that we belong to a great good, a great plan, a great community,

that reaches far beyond the range of our vision, and certainly far
beyond the limits of our understanding. For we believe that now we
know dimly, and then we will know face to face. Now God's providence is clear to us in part, then it will be known fully. Now our
calling is known to us only in part, and then it shall be known fully.

Joy and Generosity

One of my husband's favorite things about me is that I can find
any excuse to throw a theme party (for instance, enchiladas and a
viewing of the classic film *The Three Amigos*). Not that I do it all
the time, but I am prone to celebrate the little things. We always celebrate the first day of classes and the last day of classes each semester, the first day of a new job, or the fact that the weather's nice (after
a South Dakota winter, you'd celebrate nice weather, too).

But don't get the mistaken impression that I'm a bundle of fes-
tive optimism. I have warring instincts in me. Sometimes for me
seeing the glass as half empty would be looking on the bright side.
Instead, I'll see a glass that could be knocked over, broken, with
the contents spilled on the Persian rug and the shards dangerously
close to a child whom I allowed to stand up in a chair that's about
to topple. I tend to be a whiner, and I have not entirely gotten rid
of my teenage tendency to think that no one understands me.

On the other hand, there's that memory of my mom who, time
and time again, would be standing in the kitchen, talking to us kids
(she loves talking with us), when she would get all happy and recite
the first question of the old catechism:

> "What is the chief end of man?
> To glorify God and enjoy him forever!"

"Isn't that wonderful?" she would say, and you could see her savor-
ing it in her mind and heart. Mom is prone to joy. She has no problem relaxing and just appreciating the beauty of something or
someone. Like her own mother, her love of God is joyful.

So, thankfully, I have gained some skills—although I have a lot
of work to do—for embracing joy. This is not mindless, shallow
joy, either. My mother lost her father when she was a young girl.

She and my father raised four independent children. I was taught and continue to learn that joy takes openness to the goodness of human life with God and it takes time.

It's all well and good to delight in the flowers in your garden, but this joy recognizes the work and patience that went into getting them to grow. This joy embraces the existence of things beyond and outside ourselves. Look at this wonderful world! The beauty of flowers and our food that grows out of the earth. The sheer talent of athletes at their work and play, running a race. In the movie *Chariots of Fire* Eric Liddell explains to his sister, "God made me fast, and when I run, I feel his pleasure." Loving someone is full of delights, like the warmth and twinkle in their eyes when they smile at you, the enjoyment of their jokes, watching them work out their passions as they live out their own giftedness.

Christ came for abundant life. He feasted, enjoyed wedding festivities, appreciated the generosity of a woman slathering luxurious perfume over his feet. This is sensuality at its best, really feeling and tasting the good, earthy things in life. There is no doubt that Jesus Christ is for joy. He came to set free the captives, bring food to the hungry, make the lame walk. The whole point of union with God through Christ by the power of the Spirit is to free us for the joy of being human—the joy of being human with God, ourselves, and others. This is the life of joy, free for the full experience of God, of ourselves, of others, of the good creation.

Joy—true joy of union with God through Christ—leads to generosity. Joy pours forth and is contagious, like a good laugh. Generosity gives what has been received. The generous person understands that joy is not an easy or light thing—it is hard-won and quite dear. Joy contains lightheartedness, but does not end there. Generosity is the outpouring of joy for the sake of another, donating one's own self to another person. When we give out of joy and love, we give life and strength to the relationship that binds us with the one to whom we give. We offer them something of ourselves. We all know that gifts can be given because we need to or have to. Oftentimes, generosity, like other Christian virtues, becomes natural after we have practiced it, deliberately, over and over again. When we give out of our generosity we offer someone something of ourselves, and by doing that, we lift them up and celebrate them.

But generosity, like suffering, does not exist for its own sake. It is important to remember that not every *possibility* for generosity automatically *demands* generosity. A person's responsibilities must be evaluated when determining the appropriate generous action. Which gift makes sense? Why am I called to offer this at this time? Am I being responsible to myself in this gift? Do I have the resources to give this gift? Does this gift make sense in the light of what I understand to be the truth of God? Does this make sense in the context of my Christian commitments? Does this gift make sense to and for others?

Martin Luther King Jr. sought to build the "Beloved Community" in which all human beings would live in peace and reconciliation. In order to build this community, King focused on eliminating the cycle of hate and violence by way of active, nonviolent resistance. Resisters would stop hate by refusing to respond to hateful acts by returning that hate. By loving one's opponent (and King was very careful to distinguish this act of love from "liking" one's opponent), the resister dismantled the violent act and substituted love as a response. King was adamant that resisters enter into rigorous self-examination, making sure that they would be able to judge in which situations they would be able to act with love, and which situations would be too great a temptation for them toward violence. We have to think seriously when we give of ourselves for others, lest we unnecessarily destroy ourselves or others in the name of generous sacrifice. When the resisters responded to the hate of bigotry with knowing intention, they were the very models of generosity: They gave love to their enemies, recognizing their humanness, their worth, giving forth of their commitment to demands of love. This is the love that lays down its life for its friends, the love that does not count equality with God a thing to be grasped, but gives forth of itself to the point of servanthood.

Of course, this element of the civil rights movement was tested severely and the process of active, nonviolent resistance was not revealed to be some sort of romanticized, idealistic exercise. The steps of resistance demanded a lot from the resisters: They had to examine the situation and determine if resistance was really needed, what form nonviolent resistance would take, and the resisters had to examine themselves in order to make sure that they were undertaking the right actions at the right time for the right reasons in the right way.

Mary, the mother of Jesus Christ, shows us how response to God's already accomplished action can be an act of discernment and an act of generosity. In Luke 1, Mary responds to the angel's announcement by saying, "Here am I, the servant of the Lord; let it be with me according to your word." In this story, Mary's response was not reluctant, but free. She did not resign herself and merely submit; she chose to cooperate.

Her song reflects her Old Testament heritage in which she grew in knowledge of God. She agrees to this event out of gratitude to God. Mary's spirit rejoices. She affirms her relationship to God by celebrating God's love for her. She makes sense out of this bizarre event for us when she puts forth her response. Clearly, Mary does not yield to God simply because the angel has told her to do so. Mary consents to God's work because she knows God's goodness. Mary recognizes in the voice of the angel the God whom she knows. God scatters the proud, brings down the powerful, "feeds the hungry with good things," all according to God's promises. Mary gives good reasons for her actions and gives generously of herself for her own sake and for the sake of others in response to God. Although she finds herself in forces beyond her control and called by God to a plan far greater than her own life, she is not coerced. She responds to God by giving generously of her entire life.

Generosity lays a joyful foundation for the practice of forgiveness and repentance in the Christian community. Forgiveness and repentance are elements of reconciliation and thus build up and create Christian community. According to Leviticus, forgiveness and repentance and reconciliation are not merely declarations. The Year of Jubilee, for instance, is a restoration of people to their families and their land. In this return, sales may be made of land, but there is instituted a command not to cheat and make any more money than is absolutely necessary. The Year of Jubilee calls for generosity within community in response to God's call to the community. In this sense, generosity is established as something that anyone can do and is called to do, and establishes the possibility of generosity for all human beings. Integrity through interrelatedness is reestablished, and the concrete, earthly lives of human beings are cared for and recognized as willed by God.

Creativity

So how do we know in what ways we should live with joy, just what actions we should take to live generously, what steps we should follow to participate in God's providence for the divine creation? It is one thing to affirm with absolute conviction Christ's call to joy in the abundant life of reconciliation. It is another thing to live in, with, and for the goodness of human life in the midst of sin, evil, and suffering. One of the greatest gifts of God's freedom is creativity. We are not mindless automatons, we are reflections of the divine image, reflections of freedom for the other, ourselves, and God. We are reflections of the choice for joy and fellowship. Just as God creates each person uniquely and cherishes each one and cares for each one, so we too as creatures reflect this response to what is going on around us. We reflect the creativity of God, creativity for the sake of the other.

Discernment is a concept often employed by Christians to describe what it means to figure out the will of God for the goodness of creation, and some say that God's will is easily discernible. Perhaps we need to be in the right frame of mind or ask just the right question, or something else, but it is in the end easily discernible. For most of us, this is actually quite difficult. What are the steps involved? How do we teach our children to seek the will of God? What we want, very often, when we seek to do God's will or the right thing, is to have a process laid out very clearly for us. But more often than not, it seems to me, these sorts of clear-cut steps actually take us away from what God is doing in the world.

This is why it is important that we nurture creativity. Whenever we are following God's call in our lives, and whenever we perceive

God's activity, it is always within particular limits. It is limits that make creativity possible. There was this television show called *MacGyver* when I was in college. He was some sort of government agent who did supersecret work all by himself, an elite, ultra-talented—and ultra-nice—hero. With his only tool a paper clip, he could go into the desert and come back out of it having created a bomb to blow up the bad guys, gotten himself out of a maximum security prison, and fashioned an airplane that operated with the sun as its power source. Well, not quite, but it seemed that way. MacGyver always worked with what he had. In much more dramatic terms we see what real people have done: music and athletics are full of stories about parents who had nothing but did everything to help their children learn and develop their natural gifts. Jerry Rice, the greatest pass-catcher in the history of the National Football League, was a bricklayer's son. How did he practice catching? His brothers threw him bricks.

Creativity doesn't always have such glamorous ends, of course. When we respond to God in particular situations, living out the lives we have been called to live, it is sometimes a very mundane task. We may know that the path God has called us to is work in the church. And it may be that this ministry takes the form of working in a factory and teaching teenage Sunday school. Or, we may have to be creative in finding ways to deal with our teenage children. Or if we're teenagers, we may have to find creative ways to deal with our classmates.

This television commercial is a perfect example of creativity in discernment. A person somehow has to get the keys away from her very drunk friend. In the parking lot, she says,

"Wow, what a great car."

He totters and says, "Yeah, it's a '64."

"My brother has one just like it."

"Cool."

"But he never lets me drive it. Mind if I take it for a spin?"

"Sure, I guess."

And she lets out a sigh of relief as she takes the keys. Friends don't let friends drive drunk. But sometimes they have to think fast and hard and creatively to protect them and others. In this commercial, this young woman worked great goodness with a brain that was on the lookout for the safety of her friend, for others on the road, and for herself (and for the cool car).

Our resources may be limited—financially, educationally, or otherwise—but by the power of the Holy Spirit, we can act within those limits to respond to God. We may find ourselves, by the power of the Holy Spirit, transforming negative limitations into possibilities for the affirmation of human life. Creativity for Christians means that we do not ever have to give in to fatal resignation. Only God is good, and all our goodness is in God, in whom we move and breathe and have our being. There is, then, always a way to respond to goodness. Creativity is our gift to find that way.

Compassion

Saint Augustine made the point that "the citizens of the holy city of God, who live according to God in the pilgrimage of this life, both fear and desire, and grieve and rejoice." Just because we Christians await the fulfillment of the peaceable kingdom of God, we are not people who hate the world and everything of it. Passions and emotions are part of our earthly human experience. Life in the city of God is a social life, but in a fallen world where relationships can be broken by sin, by accident, and by suffering, there is no social life without pain at some level. The more friends we have, the more widely they are scattered. The joy that we have in fellowship is mixed with absence and parting. Passions are necessary when living in an earthly world because life changes from good to bad and bad to good. In a world where your mother dies, it's important to cry, for you have loved her deeply.

In fact, Augustine claims that these emotions of human existence are necessary for being human, especially as we seek to live for the goodness of God in the midst of sin and suffering. "But so long as we wear the infirmity of this life, we are rather worse men than better if we have none of these emotions at all." In recognizing the sin of the world we recognize our own, and the one "who lives without sin puts aside not sin but pardon."

The point Augustine is making is that our emotions, passions, and affections need to be ordered, not abandoned. Passions can go wrong as much as they can go well. Our anger can destroy just as it can direct us toward what is just and good and right. Our love for a human being can lead us to destructive actions or to good actions. Right ordering—learning how to be passionate in a way that affirms the goodness of God and God's creation—helps us to build our emotional, relational life in a way that reflects the divine image of individual life together for God and for others.

This is compassion, passion *with* others. In Christian terms, to be compassionate is to be passionate for others. This means sharing their grief, bearing their burdens, delighting in their delight, taking joy in their goodness. Developing our compassion recognizes the biblical image of the community of faith as the body of Christ, knowing that our health, emotional and otherwise, is bound up with that of others. Christ, in his Sermon on the Mount, urges us to the joy that leads to generosity that lives in compassion when he urges us to give our cloak to the person who sued us and took our coat. There is no standard set for who gets our compassion and who doesn't, for all have sinned and fallen short of the glory of God. Compassion—love rightly ordered for the other person—is possible because God first loves us.

6

Living in the *Imago Dei*

*L*earning how to pay attention to goodness is more easily said than done. But it is this ability to pay attention that is critical for Christians, for this is how we learn to see the world as God's creation, as reconciled to God in Christ, as a world we live for. If this is important to learn, it is certainly important to teach. And not only because it is tricky, but because we learn by being taught.

Our Calling

The good news of the gospel is that even though we are still sinners, we have been saved. Our sin has not been sanctified—evil is not OK—but we, sinners, have been restored to God and to the purpose for which God created us. As individual human beings caught up with one another in the fulfillment of our humanity, we are humble for we realize that what God has created us to do and who God has created us to be is part of so much more. Being called by God does not make us better than anyone else (for all are called and all have sinned). Being called by God makes us witnesses and servants to the glorious good news of the gospel that each human being is loved and cherished by God.

In Isaiah 43:1–13 we read the moving passages that have brought comfort and joy to so many. God calls us by name, and we are God's own. We are so precious that we will not be overwhelmed or destroyed by any disaster. From the farthest reaches of the earth the Creator calls back the people of Israel, all God's sons and daughters, all who are called by God's name. But the gathering in of God's people is not the end of the story. These people, who are precious and loved, are sent out to be God's witnesses in the world.

Likewise, in Romans 8 we are assured again that no matter how tremendous appear the obstacles to the strength of God's love, there is nothing at all anywhere in the universe that can separate us from God. Not only we ourselves, but the entire creation has been groaning in pain for the reconciliation of Christ, the apostle Paul writes. Though we experience suffering and hardship, we know that the God who chose to call us into being and give us abundant life is the God who makes that purpose come to fruition. So since we are called according to God's purpose, we know that everything works together for good.

We believe that all those whom God has created God has also called. God creates with purpose, and sustains and preserves with purpose. Our purpose unfolds in our uniqueness and it is uniquely intended for us. We share in the same calling, a calling not exhausted by simply being. The gifts and abilities with which we have been created are for the glory of God and for the sake of others, not only for our own sake.

We Christians believe that God brings together God's people, so that all these gifts may benefit one another. We are all bound up in one body, the body of Christ, who is our head. To be called by God means to be called for the sake of the world to others. Thus, calling is not restricted to someone being called as a pastor or missionary. Religious service is that kind of call and so much more. It is *any service* rendered to God and to others. We are called to one another and to God in everyday life. We enter into Christ's calling, Christ's freedom, and Christ's work. In other words, this calling, or vocation, is a part of our baptism. As we go through our day-to-day life, then, calling doesn't mean making sure we have the plan of our life exactly right. Vocation means that we take a path on which we follow God, who goes before us, calling out the way ahead.

It's like going to the Adirondacks with my family and climbing Castle Rock. And a Christian is like me, responding to the call of my family. You see, I always lagged behind, since climbing steep things was certainly not my idea of vacation, and I have never been known for my athletic prowess. They would always be ahead of me, encouraging me, telling me what was ahead, sometimes stopping to rest with me (not exactly a sacrifice for many of us Bartels, since one of our greatest joys is relaxing and enjoying the moment) and walk with me—all because they knew the top was worth getting to. A view of the Adirondack range and the lakes nestled within on a clear day is a lovely sight indeed.

Mom and Dad were right, of course. It was good for me, and much to my chagrin, I actually enjoy walks now, and it feels funny in my adulthood not to take a long walk on a Sunday. God calls out to us saying, "Yes, this is the way," and God knows that fulfilling our vocation, our calling as a disciple of Christ, is something that takes steps. These steps can be baby steps, and steps carefully placed. And yes, often we take missteps or just plain sit down and refuse to go on. The callings we see in others look grand to us from the outside sometimes, but always, from the inside, they are made up of little steps.

Surely Mother Teresa was one such person, called to a life of service as a Christian, fulfilling a vocation. But much as we noticed, across the globe, the wonder of her sacrifice for the rejected and sick and poor, only those who visited her in her hospital knew of the little steps which comprised her calling. It required lifting the heads of those who were too ill to lift themselves, and carefully pouring in the soup and water to give them nourishment. It required cleaning bedsores and remains of bodily functions, and changing bedsheets. It required walking out into the streets of Calcutta to the homeless and destitute so far beyond her doors. Teachers and nurses on a day-to-day basis respond to everyday situations, bandaging wounds, figuring out how Johnny needs to learn addition, dealing with a child's confusion or delight and corralling it for the child's welfare.

The work of teachers, nurses, and construction workers requires others working, too. For Mother Teresa, it required many additional nuns and other people. She did not do this on her own. She founded an order of workers, all called to service. All of them together contributed to this work. This is a particular path that will go on way beyond the lifetime of Teresa, and daily all these people walk it together. Mother Teresa needed these others for the order to be what it is. She lived out her freedom for others in such an interesting way. The callings of all these people come together to make something even greater than one effort on its own. We are called according to *God's* purpose, and God brings these callings together to do something wonderful. Together we make up what God intended, and that is made possible by the love of God in Jesus Christ, sealed on our hearts and minds by the Holy Spirit.

Discipleship

Our calling is a series of steps that we take as we respond to God's leading in our lives. But how do we follow Christ on this path of discipleship through the world in which we live here and now? How do we live as people in the world but not of it, as people who are of God? How can we possibly not be influenced by our culture and its values and its dynamics?

The short answer is: We can't. We are, in fact, influenced by the culture in which we find ourselves, the society of which we are a part. In this time of transition between centuries, we are affected by what is particular to our society: television, commercialism, Disney, crime, drugs, sexual mores, pluralism, relativism, fundamentalism; the list goes on and on. In the midst of this, Christians are called to be of God and not of the world. But we Christians don't have to look at this culture as anti-God in order to make ourselves pure and righteous. We don't have to be against this world in order not to be of it, and in order to be of God. The things listed above are good or bad depending on how we decide to reflect on them and respond to them in light of our obedience to God. Because of the life, death, and resurrection of Jesus Christ, we Christians know that God is at work in Christ to reconcile the world to God's own self. So when Christians look at the world, we don't see it as separate from God, let alone as against God.

This doesn't mean that we see God and the world as identical with one another. Christians are not pantheists—we don't believe that the turtle over there is God, or that we ourselves are God along with the rest of creation. We do believe that this world, which God created and called good, has been restored and reconciled by God. Likewise, when we see God, we do not see the Creator without seeing the creation at the same time. If I ponder the alleged criminal being walked in chains across my television set as anything other than the beloved child, created and called by his God, I am rejecting God and turning a blind eye. This doesn't mean that I don't take crime seriously, for as a disciple, I am horrified at the destruction and abuse of the life of God's creation. The sin of another does not remove that person from God's love, and my rejection of any part of what God has created is a rejection of God's own self.

So living as a created, called, and redeemed child of the Creator doesn't mean drawing a line in the sand and being militant about who's in and who's out. Living in the world but not of it does mean, precisely, that we love this world as God's world. How then do we know how to love this world—not on its own, as a thing apart from God, but as a thing created and sustained and loved by God?

I hesitate to use the word "love" sometimes because people often equate it with a variety of feelings and actions that are anarchic, selfish, destructive, and weak. The Christian understanding of love, while humble, is strong, not weak. So when I know that the alleged criminal walking in chains across my television screen has been arrested for molesting children, I am cautious. This is not because I am sure that the person is evil. I am cautious because my allegiance to a God of love, justice, and forgiveness means that my responsibility entails responsibility to this alleged criminal *and* to children and their parents. In other words, being loving isn't being nice: it's putting oneself on the line for the safety, joy, and welfare of others. Love is about real life, not ideas.

And so we learn from Jesus Christ, who, as fully God and fully human, lived a life of love. This life of love was not namby-pamby or wishy-washy. Any Christian idea that love avoids confrontation or looks for the easy way out has no bearing on what real life is. Christ was firm and strong: Christ forgave prostitutes (like the ones we see in our towns and cities); had meals with tax agents (the

IRS?!); and refused to allow pompous, self-righteous, law-abiding citizens to condemn a vulnerable, outcast woman. Christ overthrew money changers in the temple. Jesus Christ took people as they were, always as they were, and sent them on their way to live a new life.

How much more should we, who are not perfect, accept people as they are? We believe we have been accepted, and we take to heart and rely on the biblical assurance that Jesus came precisely for us—sinners. Understanding our life in this world and deciding how we should live then means that we recognize that people we see every day are not just numbers or nameless faces, but individuals who belong to us because they belong and are defined primarily by God and not us.

So how do we watch television? Buy clothes? Go to high school? Go to work? Baby-sit? Read the newspaper? Make medical decisions? We must discern, we must test the spirits to see what is of God. We must live in this world but respond to God, whom we believe is in this world. What is God calling us to do here and now? Who is God calling us to be here and now?

When we ask these questions about how to live as a created and called person in this world, we are committing ourselves to a major claim: God is the creator of all that is. By our actions we do not create, nor control. We reflect divine creativity in our own creative participation in God's care of the world, but only because God is the one who has enabled us to do so. We cannot make reality happen the way we want it to happen. Our actions are not independent from God. They are dependent on God. Our actions point to the God who acts, and it is God who is acting in the world, through us, for God's own purposes.

What does this mean about viewing the world? It means that when we view the world and what is going on in it, we don't separate what happens from God's presence, or from God's design. Our belief in the doctrine of providence reminds us that God is at work in the world, bringing things together. We could ask ourselves, "What is the action I should take to bear witness to the God who is working to reconcile all things to God's self?" If our actions aren't controlling actions, but responsive ones, then our understanding of the world changes dramatically. We see ourselves as witnesses, not little gods.

An example along these lines has been used often and will continue to be used often, as it should: the shooting at Columbine High School in Littleton, Colorado, in 1999. This event shocked many, as teenagers took to violence for reasons that seem unimaginable. The problem with this, of course, is that these reasons are not really unimaginable: we just thought that human tendencies to violence were well contained. More and more the media brings us evidence of violence and hatred all across our country (and we should remember that shootings have been occurring in schools for decades). It is becoming politically correct to be politically incorrect. All across our country, in our own hometowns, in the cities we live in, in the schools our children attend, in our workplaces, in all these places there is evidence of that which destroys life and is against God. How do we see it, and how do we respond to it? How do we live as people in the *imago Dei?*

Those who practice discernment as disciples of Christ need to be open to creativity. We Christians also need to remember that each human being is born into the heritage of God's activity in the world to prosper human life. Our action is limited, and it should be. God is already at work beyond us. So Christian discernment must be humble. Humility means that we recognize the limits of our knowledge, and it also means that we recognize that there is much more reality than what we know, reality in which God is present.

But how do we know what work in the world is God's and what work in the world is against God and against God's creation? In our discernment we must follow the biblical injunction to "test the spirits" and see if they are from God. This takes study of Scripture and prayer and openness. But it requires one major effort: We need to rid ourselves of as much self-deception as we can.

We are sinners, even though we are redeemed and reconciled. We will always tend to mislabel our sin. We will always tend to equate what God thinks with what we think. Sometimes we overestimate ourselves, sometimes we underestimate ourselves. We must be rigorous in trying to see ourselves clearly and not deceive ourselves. We can deceive ourselves, for instance, by saying that football is great, and isn't it wonderful when people get to use their athletic abilities to the fullest. But we fail to continue on and reject the practices that sometimes (not always) go along with the culture of football, like heavy drinking, abuse of women, and abuse of the football players' own bodies and minds. Likewise, we fail, as communities, to reject those practices that often go along with opposition to homosexual practice. A few years ago the whole country found itself facing the infamous murder of a gay man in Wyoming. Then came Matthew Shepard's funeral. People drove from a church in Kansas to march at the funeral bearing signs that read "God hates fags."

This is a situation in dire need of a testing of the spirits. The most obvious response is to point out that we deceive ourselves if we think that condemning one sin gives us license to commit another. It is unthinkable that Christians could ever hate in the name of God, but it has been happening for centuries. Less obvious is the need for testing on the part of those Christians who condemn those who carried the signs because they were not loving. How can we condemn and be loving at the same time? We must test what we see, and we must test ourselves.

When we practice discernment, we must also recognize that we share the *imago Dei*. We are bound up in a community of people who, individually and together, are all striving to live as people created in the *imago Dei*. Christian community is unified by nothing but Jesus Christ. The question is how. By recognizing this commonality, Christians take a particular stance toward the world. Affirming our belief that God has created, called, and redeemed human beings means we look at the world in a particular way. For instance, Christian vision does not allow us to see any human being as beyond God's love. If any human being is beyond God's love, that is something that God sees, not us. For our vision of the world sees the world as belonging to God: we do not look at the world *as* God.

One major element remains when we think about how we live as people who bear God's image. But first, I have a joke: There are five frogs sitting on a log. Four of them decide to jump off. How many are left? I got the answer wrong when Suzy told me this joke. I said four, but the answer is five. Just because the frog decided to jump off didn't mean it did jump off. Figuring out what we are supposed to do in response to God's call is nothing without doing it. We verify what we believe with our lives. Our lives and the lives of others are real, not mere ideas. The call from Jesus Christ to love one's neighbor entails real, everyday actions in response to our neighbor, not just agreement with the idea.

Discernment is a process by which Christians determine and live out, in their day-to-day lives, their responsibility to God, their selves, and others with whom they are in community. We have to learn how to do this, on a daily basis. We have the Ten Commandments, but we are the ones who have to live out particular commandments in particular situations. Much earlier in this book I referred to Luther's and Calvin's brilliant perception about the commandments. That is, that they are not just prohibitions for what is wrong, but indicators for what is right. So we not only refrain from stealing; we actively protect people and the things they have and need in life. Discernment is important because each situation will vary for protecting what others have in life.

Many of us were not taught in our churches to pay attention to all the nuances of the situations in which we find ourselves, to think critically and creatively. But it is vital that we learn how to teach this. Teaching itself is a hard endeavor, demanding critical and creative thinking. As a particular sort of task, teaching requires attention to the uniqueness of individuals, since all human beings are unique and learn in different ways and at different paces.

Because of the unique nature of each individual who is taught, teaching must take into consideration the particular skills, needs, situations, and gifts of that particular individual. And, because teaching is a task of the church as a community, teaching is a way in which individual believers are integrated with the community. But we are not talking about simple assimilation here, making all individuals one single mass. No; for Christians this is actually evil. The believer is not erased as an individual. In fact, the significance of teaching for the life of the individual believer is vital: We must seek to be taught to be the individual we are called to be, and likewise we must teach those around us in such a way that their individuality is brought out for their own sake as well as for the sake of God and others. How else can we clear the way (so far as it is within our power) for human beings to discover what God is calling them to, and thus clear the way for God to care for the world?

Service

In the Gospel of Mark we read the story of the healing of the paralytic. Jesus was preaching in Capernaum, and so many people heard of his return that the room was filled to overflowing. A group of people had brought someone who was paralyzed so that he could hear Jesus and be healed, but they couldn't get anywhere near Jesus. Four of them then proceeded to carry this paralyzed friend up onto the roof of the building (with no help, of course, from a motor or electric lift of any sort). Then these four people *dug through the roof,* and lowered him down until he was in front of Jesus. When Jesus saw *their* faith, he forgave the paralytic of his sins.

What audacity and perseverance and belief in Jesus Christ must have prompted this service! They dug through the roof of someone's home, they cut in line because of their single-minded pursuit of the good for their friend. In the Gospel story they are nameless, but their faith prompted Jesus to forgive the paralytic's sins. This is service. For the good of this one human being they went to extraordinary lengths so that he could receive what Jesus offered him.

This is the kind of service we are called to as Christians in all areas of our lives, and I'm as intimidated by this example as the next person. I don't know if I'm that dedicated to someone else's good. I certainly hope I would be. But the trick in paying attention to this story is not so much to compare ourselves to those friends, but to learn from what they did in their particular situation. My guess is that I won't be called on to cut through a roof to let my paralyzed friend down through. But I might be. What was it that enabled them to do this loving, caring thing?

A lot, of course, we don't know. But here are people who thought that the worth and health of their friend was so important that they risked everything to bring him to the Messiah so that he might be healed. They put the interest of someone else above their own interests, as Paul reminds us to do in his letter to the Philippians. And they had the same mind as Christ, who did not count equality with God as something to be grasped, but emptied himself, taking on the form of a servant (Phil. 2). If we are created in the image of God, and if Jesus Christ is the self-revelation of God, then we learn how to be human through Christ. This means joy, generosity, love, discipleship, and calling, and it means service to others. This means that in the particularity of our own humanness we find fulfillment as we respond to the situations in which we find ourselves, for the sake of God, others, ourselves, and the entire creation.

In the Old Testament book of Esther, Esther took on the form of a servant when Haman was hatching his plans to destroy the Jews. Talk about creativity: With the respect and dignity appropriate for the queen she was, she sought the favor of the king, with Haman, his aide, right there, inviting them to dine and tending to all their comforts. Talk about audacity: She broke convention at the risk of the king's mood and therefore at risk of her life to extend an invitation to him instead of waiting to be invited to feast together. Talk about perseverance: She stuck with her plan, even though each time she risked the king's disfavor. But what resulted was that she won him over more and more, and Haman became more and more secure in his position, until he was blindsided, not only by the fact that she knew his plans, but by the fact that she was the one the king was paying attention to. Because of her risk, her service, the king spared the Jews, and Haman's plans were foiled.

In our day-to-day lives, service, generally speaking, looks much less dramatic, much less heroic. But like the friends of the paralytic and like Esther, we are only called upon to respond, as followers of God, to what is going on around us here and now. Things that are mere habit for us—like holding the door open for someone—are services to other people. Allowing someone into line in front of us, bringing food and assignments to our fellow student, sick in her dorm room down the hall, doing the laundry for Mom and Dad, or sticking up for the kid who's always picked on are all ways that we serve.

Parents, friends, and spouses all know about the demands of love that take the shape of service. In the ordination service for Presbyterians, the person about to become ordained is asked, "Do you promise to serve the people with energy, intelligence, imagination, and love?" Service described this way admits of the varying obligations placed on us in different times and as different people, as well as the many different ways in which we can respond. Service often requires giving something up, like a night out or a weekend off. For parents it might mean no new clothes so your child gets the new outfit she needs, or taking the savings you put aside for future travel and using it so your child can go to college. Service means being patient and kind, willing to will the best for the other person.

True Christian service is done out of freedom, not duty. While we may freely choose to do our duty, it is the freedom that makes this a generous offering of ourselves to God and the other. When we force people to serve out of duty we impose on them, service is not done for the sake of the other, and it's not done for God. Nor are we the ones who know what the service is to which God is calling someone. Remember, we are not the ones who define goodness—only God defines goodness, because only God is good. Service is something we can only choose and do for ourselves in response to God and the other.

Epilogue: Life with Others before God

One of the greatest Christian slogans comes from literature: the Three Musketeers' cry of "All for one and one for all!" Of course, the Three Musketeers aren't exactly the best models for Christian life as a whole, what with all the killing and womanizing and so forth. However, for Christians, being human is beautifully summarized in this call, because we affirm that human beings were created as individuals together, free for one another, reflecting the image of the Divine who called us into being in freedom for us.

Like the musketeers, Christians understand that individuals are crucial for human life because our humanity is a social truth, not an individualistic one. So, like the friends of the paralytic, we do everything we can to make sure our friend receives healing and forgiveness. And like Esther, we willingly and deliberately put our individual selves in a position to be for the community. This is all for one, and one for all, the body that is unhealthy until every sick part, every improperly working cell, is in healthy working condition.

Unlike the musketeers, the "all" is not our small group of people to whom we are loyal. It is not "us" against "them" as it was for the musketeers, who sought to destroy the forces of the evil Cardinal Richelieu. When Christians say "all," they mean all. Our judgments of others do not determine if they are worthy of us being for them. They are worthy of us being for them because they are created in the image of God. They might be against us, but they are created in the image of God, beloved of God.

It is so easy for us to think of people we dislike or despise or disagree with as less than human, but it is just this thinking that directs our attention away from the God who called us to reconciliation in Jesus Christ. Our humanity is not determined by our mistakes or our sinfulness but by the action of God to create us, call us, and cherish us as the very image of the Divine. Each and every one of us is created in the image of God, worthy of compassion, service, providence. We are called to live fully human lives of freedom for God, ourselves, others, and the whole creation. The world would be a much better place if only people could learn to behave like human beings.

The prophet Jeremiah was trying to communicate just this point to the Israelites when he told them of God's will for them. Although they were in exile, they were to build houses, marry, have children, and plant gardens. In other words, they were to root themselves in the land where they were exiled. Babylon was God's earth just as Jerusalem was, a place worth living in, where people and green things could grow.

When we moved to South Dakota, lots of people raised their

eyebrows and made remarks about the middle of nowhere and jokes about whether or not plumbing and electricity were fully functioning (yes, they are). I suppose another way to look at it is to say that South Dakota is the middle of everywhere; just as, in a way, every place is. It just depends on where you mark the middle. I joke about South Dakota winters, and the long drives in the country where you can go for miles without seeing a single house, but I will never be able to adequately describe the beauty of this place. When I think of the beauty here, my mind's eye always recalls the deep teal of the summer skies, a deep, living blue that almost glows. And then I think of the astounding skyscapes, which I never did see back East because there was too much in the way: vivid rainbow-colored light filtering through clouds with unapologetic boldness. And then I see the grasses and the prairie flowers and the birds everywhere, by some counts more different species of birds than in any other state.

And South Dakota is the first place where I have actually gardened. People were surprised when Doug and I—two Easterners—made our move to South Dakota. Yet we heard the call to move together to this place we didn't know and to continue building our life together. We knew next to nothing about the people or the land. Our house is the first house we have owned, our first plot of earth to tend.

We set down stakes by setting down bulbs and herb seedlings, the first steps in making this place our own. When we walk out our back door during those warm summer months we can smell the basil and rosemary and the peonies when they're in bloom. Cut flowers for the house and fresh herbs for cooking are the tangible result of our first attempts at gardening. I am more surprised than anyone that I now garden a bit—as surprised as I was to make the move to South Dakota.

No less am I surprised that I continue to grow and change—in some ways to become a better person, in some ways to struggle with old concerns more strenuously. Through this people and this land I have gained glimpses of the Peaceable Kingdom, of the Garden in which God is at the center, of justice flowing like a river. All

this has been shown to me, and not least as an invitation to participate in the good existence God desires for all creation. I could not
have planned the changes in my life, my work, or my self to produce what they have produced. What is interesting is that my life
is moving forward and changing. The self that I am, whom God
created and called, and who seeks to serve, continues to be
revealed to me by God's interactions with me through this people
and this land.

We are created for joy and fellowship, called to reconciliation
and discernment, and given a life of fulfillment and service.

And God is creating us still.